# Enough About You,
# Let's Talk About Me

# Enough About You, Let's Talk About Me

## How to Recognize and Manage the Narcissists in Your Life

Dr. Les Carter

JOSSEY-BASS
A Wiley Imprint
www.josseybass.com

Published by Jossey-Bass
A Wiley Imprint
989 Market Street, San Francisco, CA 94103-1741   www.josseybass.com

Jossey-Bass books and products are available through most bookstores. To contact Jossey-Bass directly call our Customer Care Department within the U.S. at 800-956-7739, outside the U.S. at 317-572-3986, or fax 317-572-4002.

Jossey-Bass also publishes its books in a variety of electronic formats. Some content that appears in print may not be available in electronic books.

**Library of Congress Cataloging-in-Publication Data**

Carter, Les.
  Enough about you, let's talk about me : how to recognize and manage the narcissists in your life / Les Carter.
     p. cm.
  ISBN-13: 978-0-7879-8063-4 (alk. paper)
  ISBN-10: 0-7879-8063-3 (alk. paper)
  ISBN-13: 978-0-4701-8514-8 (paperback)
  ISBN-10: 0-4701-8514-7 (paperback)
  1. Narcissism. I. Title.
  BF575.N35C363 2005
  155.2'32-dc22

                                                                2005010903

Printed in the United States of America
FIRST EDITION
HB *Printing*   10 9 8 7 6 5 4 3 2
PB *Printing*   10 9 8 7 6 5 4

# Contents

Introduction     vii

**Part One: It's All About Me**     1

Chapter 1    What Makes a Narcissist?     3

Chapter 2    Why Does Someone Become a Narcissist?     23

**Part Two: Recognizing the Patterns**     43

Chapter 3    The Narcissist with an Insatiable Need for Control     45

Chapter 4    The Passive-Aggressive Narcissist     63

Chapter 5    The Bottomless Well of Common Narcissistic Demands     81

**Part Three: Dealing with the Narcissists in Your Life**     99

Chapter 6    Examining Your Anger     101

Chapter 7    Removing Fear from the Equation     121

Chapter 8    Committing to Humility     139

Chapter 9    Fostering Your Own Inner Security     157

Chapter 10   Replacing Bitterness with Forgiveness     173

The Author     193

# Introduction

My counseling career has been dedicated to learning why people struggle with anger and other troublesome emotions and how those emotions affect their relationships. When people tell me about their personal pain, I listen for the underlying patterns. Once we identify the patterns, so my thinking goes, we can begin making the adjustments in behavior and lifestyle that will provide them with the relief they so strongly desire.

One of the common troublesome patterns that I hear about is rooted in extreme self-absorption. None of us is so pure in our motives that we can claim immunity from occasional selfishness. Most of us are mature enough to acknowledge this tendency and willingly make adjustments. We learn to respond to others with respect instead of criticism, forgiveness instead of bitterness, and consideration instead of manipulation. I'm always delighted when I encounter clients who willingly take responsibility for their emotions and behaviors. As I watch them choose to contain their selfish urges, I become confident that they will indeed make lasting adjustments to their behavior that will lead to personal peace.

Through the years, however, I have seen that there are some people who stubbornly refuse to take responsibility for their disruptive behaviors. For these folks, whatever is wrong in their relationships is never about them—it's always about how other people fail or about what others are doing wrong. When I talk with them about examining their own feelings instead of resorting to blaming others, I inevitably hear a "yes, but" response. "Yes, I agree with you that something needs to change," they may say, "but how can I act differently when I'm faced with such incompetent people?" These people are masters at rationalizing, denying, and shaming their co-workers, spouses, children, friends, and families. We all know the type—the "enough about you, let's talk about me" people who are incredibly difficult to work and live with. They seldom listen to others, except to show them the error of their ways, and seem impervious to others and to their need to change. Most of them have sought counseling not to gain personal enlightenment and growth but to figure out how they can make others do what they want. Plainly put, these folks just don't get it.

When I see a client avoid personal reflection and choose to behave stubbornly and dysfunctionally, I often suspect that they have narcissistic tendencies . . . and that is not good news. By definition, narcissists are so deeply self-absorbed that they focus exclusively on manipulating other people to get what they want. They have little interest in changing, because they do not believe they have problems; it's always other people who have the problems. Generally unwilling to receive direction or feedback from managers, counselors, friends, or family members, they seem to specialize in making the lives of those closest to them miserable.

As I encounter those stuck in patterns of narcissism, I find that my efforts as a counselor produce more helpful results when I discuss strategies for change with those who have the unenviable task of living with narcissists day-in and day-out. Although it may seem unfair that those bearing the brunt of the negative narcissistic behavior should have to be the ones to change or adapt, the truth is that they are the only ones in the relationship who can change the dynamics. Since narcissists tend to think of themselves as the sane ones who must navigate through the problems that everyone else causes, they try to manipulate those around them to cater to them. If I can help their colleagues, families, and spouses learn how to evade their traps, I feel we have achieved some measure of success. In most cases, those strategies produce the only relief possible for those who are in close relationships with narcissists.

My purpose in writing *Enough About You, Let's Talk About Me* is to help you, the reader, understand the nature of narcissism so you can determine how best to manage your responses to and even free yourself from the predictable problems that accompany relationships with narcissists. Every now and then, I am pleasantly surprised when I see a narcissist who can make bona fide efforts to grow and mature, but I find that is the exception to the rule. I have found instead that if the people who live and work with narcissists can establish proper relationship boundaries and if they can follow a smart and strategic game plan for maintaining their emotional composure, they can minimize much of the anger and fear that they have experienced.

In the pages to come, then, we will explore the main narcissistic patterns of behavior and look at ways of maintaining your composure and sanity as you manage and deal with the narcissists in your life. I use many stories to show how people like you learned to face the challenge of responding to narcissists in an emotionally balanced manner. I have altered the identities of the people in these stories to protect their privacy, but they represent real people in very real circumstances.

While I get credit for being the author of this book, my efforts have been greatly enhanced by a wonderful staff of editors at Jossey-Bass Publishers, led by Sheryl Fullerton. She has provided invaluable assistance in preparing the manuscript, as has Joanne Clapp Fullagar. To say I am thankful for their efforts is a grand understatement. Little did I know how blessed I would be when I first joined the team at Jossey-Bass.

# Enough About You, Let's Talk About Me

Part One

# *It's All About Me*

## Chapter One

# What Makes a Narcissist?

In Greek mythology, so the Roman poet Ovid tells us, Narcissus was the extraordinarily beautiful son of a minor god. He was so handsome that all the nymphs of the woods, where he went often to hunt, were in love with him. But he shunned them all. One day a maiden who had tried in vain to attract him uttered a prayer that he might some time or other feel what it was to love and not have that love returned. The avenging goddess Juno heard and granted the prayer.

Soon after that, while he was out hunting, Narcissus came upon a clear fountain, with water like silver, unknown to shepherds and beasts of the forest. He stooped down to drink and saw his own image in the water. Thinking the image was some beautiful water-spirit living in the fountain, he stood gazing with admiration at the bright eyes, the rounded cheeks, the ivory neck, the parted lips, and the glow of health and exercise over all. He fell in love with him-self. When he brought his lips near to take a kiss and plunged his arms in to embrace the beloved object, it fled but returned again after a moment and renewed his fascination. Narcissus could not bear to turn away; he lost all thought of food or rest while he hov-ered over the brink of the fountain gazing longingly upon his own image. As his tears fell into the water, the image fled again and again, leaving him inconsolable. Since he could not tear himself away, by degrees he lost his color, his vigor, and the beauty that had once charmed the nymphs. Eventually he pined away and died. The nymphs mourned for him, especially the water nymphs. They prepared a funeral pyre and would have burned his body, but when they went to get it, it was nowhere to be found. In its place grew a flower, purple within and surrounded with white leaves, which bears the name and preserves the memory of Narcissus.

In recent times, the term *narcissism*, taken from the myth of Narcissus, has become associated with an exaggerated focus on and absorption in the self. If each of us were honest, we would acknowledge moments when we become so tuned-in to our own interests, yearnings, needs, or cravings that we seem unaware of what is going on outside ourselves. Haven't there been times when you took that extra unnecessary glance in the mirror or got carried away talking on and on about a favorite topic without paying attention to others' reactions? Or you might have responded to someone's personal revelation with the reply, "Oh, that reminds me of a time when I . . ." instead of focusing on that person's feelings or needs in telling you the story. Perhaps, too, you can become so engrossed in private fantasies that you momentarily lose focus on the people and events around you, or maybe you have a habit of interrupting others in mid-sentence. Self-absorption is enormously common and easy to lapse into.

Beyond these occasional ordinary ways in which we are preoccupied with ourselves, however, are behavior patterns that so thoroughly dismiss the interpersonal dimension that they are toxic. People with a full narcissistic behavior pattern are so completely, even pathologically self-absorbed that they lack empathy, can be thin-skinned, and demonstrate very low levels of true awareness of themselves or others.

While it is amusing to consider the ancient story of a teenage boy falling hopelessly in love with his own reflection, it is far from amusing when you are forced to live, work, or associate with individuals who seem endlessly and obliviously self-absorbed. Whether in marriage, in the extended family, in social circles, in civic or church organizations, or at work, narcissists have a way of frustrating those trying to relate to them. While they often seem friendly or gregarious during the beginning phases of a relationship, time inevitably reveals that they are genuinely disinterested in most things beyond their own agendas. As they maintain that self-focus, their desire to manipulate and control for their own purposes can elicit rage, hurt, disillusionment, confusion, false guilt, tension, intimidation, and insecurity in others around them.

A high percentage of the people who come to me for counseling reveal that their problems have been either instigated or greatly worsened by very selfish or manipulative people. Their lives have become intertwined with ones who are deceptive, phony, unwilling to change, controlling, and oblivious to their needs. They ask me, "How can I get this person to change?" Then I tell them, "There's very little you can do to persuade a true narcissist to change. By definition, narcissists have a very low ability to incorporate someone else's version of reality because they see themselves as the ultimate keepers of truth. They admit no wrong, or if they ever do admit wrong, it is only a matter of time before they convince themselves they were actually right." While my clients know that my response is probably correct, they nonetheless feel great angst about it.

Cindy, who admitted being worn out by her soon-to-be ex-husband, Martin, was one of those clients. Although she was only in her mid-forties, she looked older than her age, and she described that much of her adult life had been spent "on the end of a yo-yo string." She had once been a confident, eager young woman who seemed to be going somewhere in her life, but by the time she came to see me she said she felt herself to be just a shell of that person.

"When Martin and I began dating," she recalled, "I was fresh out of college and had a wonderful job in the mortgage business. I was making lots of good contacts in the real estate world, and despite my young age I was gaining the confidence of influential people. When Martin came along I could tell right away that he was a real charmer. I knew he had a history of dating several high-profile women, and something told me to steer clear of him. One of his best buddies pulled me aside and told me to believe only half the stories he told about his successes, and he even warned me not to get serious with him. Like a foolish schoolgirl, though, I fell for Martin's wit and charm, and before you knew it, I had an engagement ring on my finger. He told me how much he adored me and how he would spend the rest of his life trying to make me happy. Those were words I really wanted to hear, and it never occurred to me to disbelieve him. He seemed so sincere."

Heaving a big sigh, she continued. "It didn't take long for me to realize that he was an incredibly selfish man. I had no illusions that marriage would be rosy, and I was prepared for a fair exchange of give and take; I knew we would have to negotiate differences along the way. Right from the start, though, I learned that he had already determined how life was supposed to play out, so instead of working with me to find harmony, he made it his self-appointed duty to get me onto his page. He was very critical, and I soon realized whenever we had to manage conflicts, my opinion was of zero consequence to him. He disregarded my feelings entirely, then he'd try to force me to see the light of his ways."

"How would he do this?" I asked.

"Well, his tactics varied. Sometimes he would argue and argue until he finally wore me down. Other times he would punish me with silence, knowing that was torture to me because I like closure. Other times he would just secretly do what he wanted to do behind my back. Frequently he would lie or at least distort the truth." Then Cindy paused before she went on. "I cannot recall one time when he told me I had a good point or that he was wrong. I felt consistently belittled by him, and over time I began to question my own sanity." With another sigh, she said, "Living with that man was a nightmare."

More often than not, the narcissists are not the ones who make their way into my counseling office. Though they usually have deep histories of anger and broken relationships, they rarely think they are the ones who need help. Sometimes they come in for a few sessions, but it is usually because they want to prove the other person wrong or to persuade me to validate their notions or their manipulation of the other person. Every now and then narcissists will make genuine efforts to change their ways, if they come to the point where they no longer have the energy left to perpetuate their former lifestyle. Regrettably, these cases are the exception rather than the rule.

Instead, those in relationship with narcissists are usually the ones who want to learn about narcissism. Like Cindy, they have had to admit the futility of trying to force change that will not occur. They have come to realize that they have to maintain their own emotional healthiness, even if the narcissist remains in a toxic state. I encourage these people to become as thoroughly educated as they can about the pattern they are up against. Only by learning to evaluate their circumstances objectively can they begin to manage the subjective elements within them—and the narcissistic patterns of the person who is creating so many difficulties in their lives.

## Common Narcissistic Traits

Narcissism is so powerful that it can be displayed in a broad variety of behaviors and personality types. In the coming chapters, we will examine ways to respond to its various manifestations and patterns, but first, let's acknowledge the eight primary ingredients common to a narcissistic pattern of behavior:

1. An inability to empathize; that is, an inability to experience another person's feelings and perceptions from that person's point of view
2. Manipulative or exploitive behavior
3. A sense of entitlement
4. An inability to receive direction
5. An insatiable need for control
6. A haughty or judgmental spirit
7. An unwillingness to acknowledge reality
8. An ability to create favorable public impressions

This list is not a flattering depiction of any person, yet these traits are highly predictable in narcissists. Those who must relate to narcissists, therefore, need to gain an objective understanding of these traits, so they can keep a handle on the emotions that the behavior arouses, especially because most narcissists are highly skilled at convincing those around them that they (not the narcissists) are defective. Under a narcissist's steady repetition of criticisms, others' confidence and resolve can erode. That's why it is so essential to understand narcissistic tendencies fully.

For the sake of clarity, let's examine the eight narcissistic traits one by one.

### It's All About Me: Lack of Empathy

No two people can ever be expected to reason, feel, or prioritize in the same way. In a stroke of pure genius, our Creator chose to endow each person with his or her own uniqueness, right down to the very DNA that is the blueprint for each living organism. Healthy relationships, then, begin with the recognition (or perhaps it would be more poignant to call it the celebration) of the differences that are bound to surface in each interaction.

Each difference in a relationship represents an opportunity for the participants to grow and stretch. People who are not narcissistic recognize this basic truth. For instance, in an ordinary situation, if a non-narcissistic co-worker notices that you handled a project contrary to her preferences, she will not necessarily be upset. She will consider the possibility that the co-worker has a different and equally valid perspective, whereas a narcissist will dismiss another's preferences or feelings as irrelevant. A healthy response to such a situation would be, "I want to understand you better," whereas the narcissistic response would be, "You're wrong to think or feel that way."

When people differ, they can choose to be *empathetic*—to experience another's feelings and perceptions from that person's point of view. Empathy requires us to step outside of our own agendas long enough to develop an understanding of the other person's perspective. It can rightly be stated that no relationship will be whole without ongoing displays of empathy.

As I spoke with Cindy about her relationship with Martin, she told me, "Whenever we did not see eye to eye, which was often, it seemed that Martin made it his job to persuade me that my feelings were ridiculous and that he was the only one whose feelings mattered. Also, if I was just telling him about something that happened to me during the day, he would interrupt and begin talking about himself, as if my experiences meant nothing. Life was all about him. I don't think it ever dawned on him that I was a normal person who needed to feel heard and understood."

With a fiery look in her eyes, she said, "After many, many times of him dismissing my feelings, I once blurted out in sarcasm that it must be awful for him to live with someone whose feelings were always inappropriate. And do you know what he said back to me?" I didn't reply because she was clearly on a roll. "He paused for a moment and then he said I was right . . . it really was terrible having to live with someone whose emotions were so consistently off base. Not once could he conceive that my feelings had merit. Not once!"

That's the way narcissists think. Because they cannot muster an understanding or sympathetic reaction to others' emotions or concerns, they generate great frustration as they rationalize that the world would be a much better place if others would just quit being so wrong in the ways they feel and react. They do not consider the pain they inflict on others, nor do they give any credence to others' perceptions. They simply do not care about thoughts and feelings that conflict with their own.

### I Want What I Want: Manipulative or Exploitive Behavior

Psychologically healthy people generally seek to be genuine, which involves a commitment to internal and external consistency. Simply put, *genuineness* means that someone's behavior can be trusted as an accurate reflection of that person's inner beliefs and priorities.

Narcissists are not genuine. The ways they publicly present themselves are not necessarily true representations of what they really feel or believe. They are more interested in posturing for favorable reactions than being known as authentic. Rather than understanding relationships as safe havens where openness and transparency can be practiced, they enter relationships looking for ways to coerce others to do their bidding. Narcissists replace fair and honest exchanges with behaviors that manipulate other people so that they can get their way.

One man, Jeff, described how he had learned to be cautious whenever he was in the presence of his sister, Lana. "I'm always watching my back whenever we have family get-togethers," he explained. "Lana can act as if she's your best pal, but I've learned that I can't let my guard down when she's friendly because history tells me that she's just setting me up for some manipulative purpose." For instance, as Jeff's extended family made preparations one year for a Thanksgiving Day gathering, Lana was most agreeable as she discussed her role in providing food. As Jeff put it, "Her cooperation seemed eerie because she has such a strong reputation for being argumentative or contrary regarding these sorts of things." Sure enough, as the Thanksgiving Day festivities wound down, Lana pulled her brother aside and said, "I need to ask a favor from you. My family has planned to go skiing over the Christmas break, and I'm going to need you to keep my dogs. Also, Grandma asked if she could stay with me for a couple of weeks, but since I'll be gone, I told her she could stay with you."

Right then Jeff understood why his sister had been cooperative with their Thanksgiving plans. She had two large, high-maintenance six-month-old puppies, and she did not want to pay to have them boarded. Jeff also knew that Lana often complained about attending to their Grandma's health needs, so Lana clearly did not want to have Grandma as a guest. Jeff realized that Lana had been buttering him up so he would agree to take on the chores she wanted him to do. She failed to consider that keeping the dogs would be difficult for him, given the fact that he and his wife had a newborn son, and that his wife was allergic to animal hair. Lana only cared about her needs and preferences.

The manipulations of narcissists know no limits. Sometimes the exploitive behavior takes on the form of false friendliness, as in the case of Lana's dealings with Jeff. Other times, narcissists will resort to making others feel guilty. For instance, when Lana sensed that Jeff was less than enthusiastic about doing her bidding, she listed three or four favors she had done for him recently. She assumed that if she couldn't reason with him, guilt might be a successful hook. Some even lack a conscience to prevent them from lying or conveying only partial truths. Others manipulate through pouting, giving others the silent treatment, being secretive or stubborn, conniving behind others' backs, or being intimidating. Whatever the means, their behavior indicates that they place no value on open, straightforward communication; their only concern is that they get their way.

### "You Owe Me": A Sense of Entitlement

Underlying the manipulative behavior of narcissists is a belief that they are entitled to have others do whatever they want or need. "While I'm not concerned about your needs," they might reason, "it is very important that you meet mine." When others do not do their bidding or give them the treatment they think they deserve, narcissists can be highly offended. They may respond angrily, with threats, strong pleading, or irrational criticism.

Cindy described how Martin's spirit of entitlement affected their attempts to iron out disagreements during their marriage. "It was fairly common that we would disagree on a broad range of subjects," she told me. "Naturally, Martin would explain his opinion, then I would tell him mine. Many times he would tell me that my opinions made no sense and that I should go along with his logic. I would counter that there are two sides to every argument and try to get him to see that we would have a better marriage if we could each consider what the other said and felt. He would often blurt out, 'But I'm the husband.' Somehow he felt his position in the family meant I was supposed to cater to him, and he should never lower himself to serve or understand me." When Martin sensed that Cindy might not bow to his demands, he demeaned her with cursing and shouting, sometimes following her through the house as she tried to find relief. "He was a tyrant," she told me through tears, "and he would not let me rest until I agreed with him. I grew to hate him, and I actively looked for ways to avoid him."

"What have you done for me lately?" is a common theme for narcissists. Another one is "You owe me." They can have such a strong belief that they are especially unique that they can be genuinely shocked when others choose not to grant them favored status. For instance, after Lana asked her brother, Jeff, to keep her dogs and care for their ailing grandmother, she was caught off guard when Jeff told her it would not be practical to do so. Her response to him was, "How can you do this to me? Do you realize that you're going to ruin my ski trip?" She acted deeply offended and showed no concern for his feeling that his newborn child took precedence over her dogs; in fact, she seemed totally unaware of the unreasonableness of her request.

Healthy relationships make room for interdependence, where individuals understand that they need to consider each other's goals and perspectives as they live their lives together. We can achieve balance when we discard the entitlement mentality in favor of an attitude of fairness and inclusion. Narcissists, however, have difficulty reining in their need for entitlement, making it difficult for them to expect anything other than special treatment.

### Nothing Goes In: Inability to Take Direction

There is no ongoing relationship in which the participants are so perfectly attuned to one another that there is no need for coaching and suggestions. In marriage, for instance, husbands and wives sometimes misread the other's thoughts or intentions, and, if they are mature, they agree to communicate their differences constructively. Likewise, parents and children shift and adjust their responses to each other as they age and grow. In business and organizational relations, members have to keep each other informed about changing plans and procedures. Friendships and extended family interactions also require well-coordinated back and forth exchanges as everyone's separate needs become evident and must be accounted for. Relationships are never so static that they require no adjustments, nor are they ever so complete that they allow for no mistakes.

That reasonable picture of give and take in relationships, however, does not work for narcissists. They reason that cooperation leads to imposition, and they have great difficulty with conversations or interactions that challenge them to set aside their preferences. When faced with someone who indicates that change is in order or that mistakes need to be corrected, the narcissistic response is, "You don't really expect *me* to change, do you?" The need to be special is so central to narcissists that they repeatedly lie to themselves about their own importance, and they cannot accept the notion that others might not see them the same way. Self-preservation is the narcissist's highest priority, and if it requires them to dismiss any input that might seem uncomfortable or rejecting, so be it.

Cindy mentioned how she had tried many times to talk with Martin about making adjustments in managing their many differences and conflicts, yet he repeatedly rebuffed her. For instance, she told me that during their marriage she felt they had a habit of socializing only with his friends, and when opportunities arose to spend time with her friends he would opt out. As she pled with him to accept her friends, he would say something like, "I'm not doing anything wrong," or "Those people aren't my type." When Cindy argued that he needed to be more cordial and open-minded, he would retort with something like, "Why should I stand here and listen to your whining?" or "I'll not have you telling me who I should spend time with."

She went on to explain, "After several years with him, I began recalling one time after another when I would try to talk with him about being flexible or about hearing my thoughts. In every instance he challenged me and spoke to me in a pushy tone of voice. It didn't matter what subject I talked about; his natural reaction was to treat me as if I didn't know what I was talking about. I swear, that man is the most stubborn person I've ever met. He can't learn anything new, and he can't make any changes because in his mind, he needs no change!"

Cindy finally left the marriage because Martin was so hard-hearted that no rational discussion or pleading would cause him to reconsider his behavior, even on the simplest of matters. Like most narcissists, defending his own turf was of higher priority than receiving input from his wife, even if it meant he had to defy logic in the process.

### My Way or the Highway: Insatiable Need for Control

Any relationship requires order and organization. Accountability, structure, and predictability provide security and allow the participants in a healthy relationship to learn to rely on one another to contribute positively to their mutual goals and objectives. Order and organization mean that they also must recognize the need to exercise some control over their behaviors and impulses. Healthy people willingly acknowledge that it is best to have a general plan of action as they participate with others in life's pursuits.

Narcissists, too, agree that it can be good to have controls within relationships, but they assume that they (and no one else) should be the ones holding the reins of power. For narcissists, it's not good for others to be in control because their desires might not be fulfilled under others' leadership. That's why narcissists unilaterally appoint themselves as the final authority. They dislike the idea of being submissive, but they relish the thought of others submitting to them.

One man, James, told me of a failed business venture that had been doomed due to the lack of cooperation from his partner, Philip. "I had the money," James told me, "and Philip had the contacts. We had a specialty product that could be easily marketed to manufacturers of circuit boards. From the very beginning of our efforts, though, when Philip and I met to discuss each week's marketing strategies, it became clear that there would be one way and only one way for us to proceed—and that was Philip's way. I would talk with him about my ideas, and we would seemingly have an agreement, but Philip would later conduct business as if our conversation had never occurred. When I talked with him about staying coordinated with our plan, he would just argue. It didn't take long for me to realize that he was a totally self-centered man who had used me in order to get my financial resources. Nothing I said mattered to him because he had such a need to be in control that he could justify any of his decisions. He'd go behind my back with office staff and customers, giving directives that were inconsistent with our agreements. He was bossy and critical, and no one's opinion mattered except his own."

Narcissists display their need for control through various means. Some use obvious behavior like being forceful, strident, bossy, bullying, stubborn, or argumentative. Others may use more covert behavior such as punishing withdrawal, feigning agreement, slandering others, withholding cooperation, or using seductive charm. Whatever the tactic, they are determined not to let someone else establish the rules of engagement. So convinced are they of the superiority of their ways that they cannot and will not play second fiddle. They continually look for ways to force themselves upon others.

### You're So Wrong: A Haughty or Judgmental Spirit

What makes an orchestra sound so appealing? Various instruments harmonize their distinctive sounds. A violin is distinct from a trumpet. An oboe sounds nothing like the bass drums. A piccolo is very dissimilar from a cello. A clarinet bears no resemblance to a trombone. The goal of an orchestra is not to get all the instruments to make the same sounds; rather, the aim is to blend the instruments' sounds to create a pleasing whole. Suppose the first violin speaks up and says, "What is wrong with that bassoon over there?

It's the oddest-looking object you ever saw and makes the strangest sound. Get it out of here. And what about the viola? Is that thing trying to sound like me? I certainly hope not. . . . Shoot it! And whose idea was it to let that stupid flute in here? I hate flutes! They're too perky, and they add absolutely nothing to what I'm trying to do."

This absurd analogy provides an accurate image of the judgmental way that narcissists think. In every venue they encounter people who look, reason, and set priorities differently. While common sense tells us that it is quite possible to find harmony in the midst of such differences, that's not what narcissists think.

Psychologically healthy people understand that every person is a unique blend of skills, accomplishments, and inclinations, and we are all worthy in our own right. They dismiss judgments and claims of superiority and instead openly applaud the equal value of each person. Narcissists, however, find that no one is as good (or smart or successful or skilled) as they are, and they are quick to let others know how they fall short.

As Jeff described to me how he had struggled for years to get along with his sister, Lana, he said, "From our childhood years until now, Lana has shown a relentless tendency to judge me. If she comes to my house, it takes no time at all for her to point out what's wrong with my kids, and she traces their quirks to my poor parenting skills. She doesn't like the pictures hanging on my walls. She thinks I have poor taste in music. She thinks I'm an idiot because I like to referee Little League baseball games. There is hardly anything in my life that avoids her scrutiny!"

Lana's narcissistic thinking causes her to interpret differences in comparative or competitive terms rather than appreciate them. Her approach toward life does not allow her to see her brother's distinctive traits as merely indicators of separate yet equal qualities. Her vanity causes her to denigrate Jeff for the things that make him uniquely Jeff. Her need to punish and criticize him whenever she finds him lacking reveals the depth of her judgmental thinking and her assumption that he should defer to her.

This tendency to judge differences harshly is perhaps most painful when another expresses emotions openly. For example, if a person says they feel hurt, the narcissist might reply, "Well, that's just stupid." In response to a valid expression of anger, the reply might be, "I can't believe you think that way; you're wrong." Rather than receiving personal disclosures at face value, narcissists tend to measure them against a standard of right and wrong that they have established. If you don't agree with their assessment, you're liable to receive a condescending response.

### The Truth According to Me: Unwillingness to Acknowledge Reality

In a sense, narcissists are out of touch with reality. They are not mentally ill, like a psychotic; they are just unwilling to acknowledge truth that does not match their preferences. While normal people can weigh events rationally and draw fair conclusions about themselves and others, narcissists do not. They lack the objectivity to live with reasonable insight, because their need for self-exaltation does not allow them to accept that their perceptions might not be ultimate truth. Their idealized view of themselves blinds them as they try to make sense of life, particularly the elements in themselves that might be imperfect or that might require adjustments (and they never want to make adjustments).

On many occasions in her marriage to Martin, Cindy had attempted to talk with him about his lighting quick temper. Instead of considering her input, Martin would often say something like, "If you put me up against any other man, you'll find that I have far more balanced emotions than any of them." Cindy would try to explain that she was not wanting to talk about the anger of other men, just his. But she got nowhere in her discussions because he would inevitably talk about himself in such lofty, comparative terms that he failed to acknowledge that he truly had an anger problem.

No one is without faults. That is not a truth that should create undue stress or shame; it is simply an unavoidable fact. If we can admit our faults with humility, good things can happen. If we make excuses for our flaws and think we're perfect, we not only miss the growth potential in life's lessons, we also fail to accept facts at face value. We are lying to ourselves and living without insight about our real character. Jesus Christ himself spoke the well-known phrase, "You shall know the truth, and the truth will set you free." As narcissists ignore truth and invent their own alternative realities, they are not free but imprisoned by their own falsehoods. Over time, it becomes a prison they cannot escape.

### Lethal Charm: Ability to Create Favorable Impressions

This eighth ingredient of narcissism might seem odd. How can such thoroughly disagreeable, difficult people be charming? Despite the destructive nature of this personality profile, many narcissists have a history of appearing friendly and agreeable—at first. Only after people have ongoing exposure to the private world of a narcissist do they experience the pain such a person can cause. Narcissists seem to know that if they display their selfishness too quickly, they will be shunned, so they keep it under wraps until they have gained a foothold in another's life. But it catches up with them. As narcissists age, they leave behind an ever-expanding list of relationships that ended in utter disillusionment and futility. Despite their general disinterest in others' feelings, narcissists yearn to be admired; they need to win others' approval, even as they posture to keep a manipulative edge. They become masters at feigning interest, when in fact they are not interested at all. They can cover contempt for someone with seemingly genuine friendliness. So skilled are they at appearing likeable that even close associates can be fooled into assuming that all is well in the relationship even when it is not.

James, the man who joined forces with Philip in the failed business venture, explained how foolish he felt because he had originally been convinced that they would have an ideal partnership. "I had known Philip casually for several years prior to going into business with him," he said, "and he always seemed like a nice guy. We even played golf together a couple of times, and I really enjoyed his company. It was only after we began working together that I recognized how much of a conniver he was. With his friendliness and seemingly believable promises, I had been led to assume that he would be a real joy to work with." Then, shaking his head, he added, "Boy, do I feel duped."

Likewise, Cindy reminisced about her dating days with Martin and drew a similar conclusion. "As we dated, I could tell that he was not the open-minded person that I might have wished for. I mean, he was pretty opinionated and liked being in charge, and I suppose that should have raised some red flags, but at the same time I didn't worry about it. He was also very attentive, and he acted like a gentleman, and eventually that won me over." Running her hands through her hair, she mused, "If I only knew then what I know now."

Part of the narcissistic hidden strategy is to protect the self's interests even if it means being phony. Like a wolf seeking sheep to prey upon, they can cloak themselves in ways that draw others into a trusting response, only to reveal the extent of their self-absorption at a later time.

## Your Response: Delicate Detachment

When faced with the ongoing challenge of life with a narcissist, people commonly experience a broad spectrum of emotions. Narcissism represents personal immaturity at its worst, so it is only natural for you to feel great tension as you try to determine how to respond to the manipulative behaviors that are sure to come your way. When I counsel with individuals such as Cindy, James, or Jeff, I begin with the assumption that they will only aggravate their distress if they attempt to change the narcissist. In most cases, it won't happen. Narcissists have such poor insight into their maladaptive behaviors that any efforts to get them to see the light will likely turn into arguments that go nowhere. Simply put, trying to persuade a narcissist to become non-narcissistic is an exercise in futility.

Cindy had tears in her eyes as she sat in my office reflecting on her past experiences with Martin. "That man absolutely did not know me, nor did he care to learn about my needs and feelings. I felt on guard constantly because I never knew what kind of stunt he would pull next. It seemed like our house was a courtroom, and he was the prosecuting attorney who was persistently accusing me of breaking his laws. Whenever we had conflict, we could never just talk it out like two levelheaded adults. Instead, there was blame, stubbornness, and irritability."

"How would you typically react to your conflicts with Martin?" I asked.

"I'd usually start out trying to be rational, but he had such a knack for twisting everything I said that I'd quickly become agitated and defensive. That man knew how to push my buttons, and despite my promises to myself to stay calm, I'd eventually be hooked, and the results were not pretty."

Cindy's sense of futility represents the norm for those in relationships with narcissists. Most people enter relationships hopeful and optimistic, anticipating a certain degree of respect and understanding. That optimism can quickly fade, though, as the narcissist repeatedly refuses to engage in ways that promote camaraderie.

When you are dealing with a narcissist, your task is to maintain enough emotional separation so you can stay proactive, as opposed to reactive, in your efforts to be an emotionally stable person. While you might wish that it were otherwise, you will need to proceed with the realization that you can maintain emotional integrity without the narcissist's cooperation. The narcissist does not have to set your pace.

People who find themselves in regular contact with a narcissist typically struggle with two common emotions: fear and anger. The fear might take the form of insecurity or anxiety, but it is most commonly displayed as defensiveness. The anger can show itself through rage or aggression, but it most likely is manifested in an ongoing battle with frustration, impatience, and a sense of futility.

To keep these emotions from ruling you, you will need to learn *delicate detachment*. By suggesting that you detach, I mean that it is wisest to remember that the narcissist is not the keeper of ultimate truth. You can choose to chart your own course of life even if it goes against the narcissist's preferences (and it inevitably will). You will need to separate yourself from the narcissist's agenda and be firm and resolute as you set your own course for each day. You cannot afford to depend on the narcissist to establish your life's direction.

By *delicate* detachment, I mean that your resolve to be separate need not be accompanied by a spirit of haughtiness or combativeness. The narcissist is likely to feel offended when you choose not to comply, yet that is not your problem to solve. If you can maintain a calm, deliberate manner, free of defensiveness, you can make the choices that are best for you, knowing that you are not obligated to debate those choices with the narcissist in your life.

In the following chapters, we will explore in greater detail how you can learn to detach and monitor your responses to narcissism. It will be crucial that you develop an appropriate plan of action, since the lack of planning could result in you becoming just as self-absorbed as your narcissistic antagonist. That is a possibility we would like to avert completely.

As we explore your responses to narcissism, we will continue gaining insight into the behaviors associated with this personality type, and we will examine the causes for people developing such a manner of life. In Chapter Two we will begin delving into the origins of the narcissistic pattern.

*Chapter Two*

# Why Does Someone Become a Narcissist?

You've just learned that your sister has breached your confidence and slandered you to a mutual friend. When you confessed a major blunder to her, you assumed she'd keep it to herself, but now you find out that she has told your friend all the sordid details. You feel humiliated. As you fume about this turn of events, you recall that she has treated you in the same disdainful manner many times before. You wonder, "What is it about me that draws out the very worst from my sister?"

At work, you need the help of one of the clerical staff. You talk to him about how he can assist you, but he just rolls his eyes as he rudely says, "You'll just have to take a number; everyone wants a piece of me today." Normally you would be patient in such a situation, but you realize that this guy has dismissed you many times before, and you know that he has a reputation for going his own way with little regard for the rest of the team. You wonder, "Have I done something to get on his black list? Why does he always seem to have it in for me?"

As you find yourself entangled with the narcissists in your life, it is normal to look inward and ask, "Why is this person treating me this way? What did I do to deserve this?" While it is reasonable to want answers to your questions, you can mistakenly take responsibility for the other person's shortcomings. This is exactly what the narcissist wants you to do.

To practice the delicate detachment that is so necessary as you engage with a narcissist, you will need to be aware that his or her behavior is rooted in earlier experiences that have nothing to do with you. Because narcissists would act the same way regardless of what you do, it's nearly impossible to have any control over them. As you understand where narcissistic patterns come from, you can free yourself from feeling like you have to fix them or try to generate an increasingly elusive harmony.

## We All Begin as Narcissists

Although it might sound a little harsh, I begin with the assumption that each of us starts life with the potential to become narcissistic. None of us is so pure that we are completely free of raw and rampant selfishness. Rather, every one of us is a mixture of both positive and negative traits—and that is evident from a child's earliest years.

Nothing can generate smiles quite like young tots who are playful and cuddly. Their innocence and friendliness can get even the crustiest soul to start cooing and playing and talking silly. Playing simple games with youngsters and sharing grins and laughter can be pure ecstasy. When they're in a cooperative mood, small children can bring out the best in adults, who are just waiting for an excuse to be tender and nurturing.

As cute as very little children can be, though, we all know they also have another, less appealing side. We've all seen young ones throwing temper tantrums or being generally unruly; it can be quite ugly. It can be amazing how many times in a day a toddler can say no. Their general tendency to focus on what interests them rather than on what needs to be done—like a bath or bedtime—can be just as frustrating. If you put several toddlers in a room together for any significant length of time, the possibility for conflict, anger, rude behavior, and tears increases exponentially. Those caring for toddlers at their worst might find themselves also feeling impatient and irritable—it's natural, given how hard it is to manage a child's behavior when he or she is completely self-absorbed.

No matter how sweet or loving children might seem, their unmitigated selfishness can appear at any time, with no advance warning or logic. No child ever needs tutoring to learn how to be demanding, defiant, obstinate, tuned out, whiny, or willful. The me-first mentality is so predictable and universal that, truly, none of us begins life without it.

How does this pure self-absorption become such a central feature in a little child's disposition? In part, the beginnings of narcissism can be traced to the growing child's unmet emotional and psychological needs; we will examine these in the next several pages. Yet while we can attribute selfishness to such ingredients as lost parental love, early life trauma, or unmet needs, there is another ingredient that the psychological community is often uncomfortable with. It is the issue of original sin. Young children's selfishness and self-absorption are too pervasive and instinctive to be due only to environment and upbringing. In his landmark book *Whatever Became of Sin?* prominent psychiatrist Karl Menninger lamented that with the advent of modern psychology, the word *sin* has been left out of our considerations of what is wrong with the human condition. When Menninger and others (myself included) assert that a person possesses a *sin nature*, we mean that there is something intrinsic to an individual's character that predisposes him or her to do wrong. Traits such as self-absorption and haughtiness cannot be attributed to outside influences alone. They exist as a by-product of an inherently flawed spirit. Throughout our lives we have to work with our innate flawed nature, examining our souls and learning to take responsibility for living consistently with godly character. Psychological insights have their place in deciphering emotional ailments, but they are incomplete without simultaneously addressing the spiritual dimension.

The upside of acknowledging sin as a contributor to our personal flaws and faults is we can take responsibility for our character. "The reason I am a manipulator," the common reasoning goes, "is due to a history of unmet needs." While I do not argue that environmental problems contribute to adult deficiencies, I do not lay all psychological problems at the feet of mother, father, spouse, and other significant people. Instead, we can develop a fuller understanding of the human condition when we draw upon both the theological and psychological explanations for maladaptive lives.

Judeo-Christian theologians (those who study God and God's role in the human affairs) explain that every individual's natural instinct to do wrong can be traced to Adam and Eve's decision to defy God, to eat of the Tree of Good and Evil (something God had forbidden). In doing so they elevated themselves over God. The doctrine of original sin asserts that the first humans had the option to live according to God's rules of right and wrong but chose their own rules instead. Personal cravings took center stage, while submission to God's guidance was relegated to a lesser role. The resulting selfishness became integral to human nature and has been passed along to all generations that followed.

Whether you regard the Garden of Eden story as truth or fiction, it's a contradiction of reality to deny that tendencies toward unhealthy self-absorption are a fixed presence in each personality, as demonstrated in history and everyday experience. Christian writer C. S. Lewis summarized the problem of original sin by asserting that a universal law of right and wrong exists in every person's mind, yet each individual chooses to behave contrary to that law simply because he or she can. The tendency to make ourselves gods is on display in all of us from the point when we can make our own conscious choices. There has never been a time in history when this was not so.

When we witness small children raging, pouting, disobeying, and acting out in other ways, we might smilingly regard it as childish immaturity, yet it is more than that. It is also an indication of an inability to consider others' needs and feelings because of an extreme focus on the self that is the hallmark of original sin. When we say a child is maturing, we mean that he or she is growing in capability and willingness to submit to a higher order of goodness. While we all begin with the sinful inclination to be insensitive toward others' needs, with training and nurturing, we can grow out of that phase, nurturing traits such as empathy and consideration.

Narcissism, then, is not defined by the presence of selfishness (since this is common to every person), but by the inability to shed that selfishness as the central feature of one's nature. (We'll be talking more about this in Chapter Eight.)

When young people grow into adults who have not successfully managed their core selfishness, it is predictable that there were patterns in childhood development that hindered maturity. Emotional needs and life skills were not properly addressed, leaving them stuck in the self-absorption that is so common in young children. Learning about narcissists' psychological deficiencies can keep you from carrying the burden of their troubled relationship baggage.

## The Legacy of Unmet Psychological Needs

In addition to inborn selfish nature, environmental and developmental factors can also help to shape a child into a narcissistic adult. If you want to respond constructively to narcissistic behavior, it's important to understand the unmet psychological and emotional needs—around intimacy, self-esteem, privilege, power, control, and moral integrity—that contribute to it. We'll be talking about all of them in this chapter. While you might never succeed in getting the narcissists in your life to change, insight into how they got that way can foster an objectivity that can keep you from getting unnecessarily ensnared by their selfish behavior. As you learn that their adult behavior is influenced first by inborn and then second by environmental influences, you will see clearly that their misbehaviors are rooted in problems that you did not cause.

### A Lack of True Intimacy

In order to develop emotional maturity, children need years of satisfying and intimate connections with those around them. Beginning with their relationships with their mother and father, young children need consistent messages of affirmation and understanding. If children receive steady messages of love and concern from their primary caregivers, they slowly begin to recognize that there is a grand world beyond them, one where their emotions and needs do not always come first. When they learn to trust their parents, siblings, friends, teachers, and others who are significant in their lives, they eventually accept the reality that their own perceptions are not the only ones worthy of consideration. Bonding, then, is the bedrock of an empathic spirit.

By definition, narcissists do not deeply ponder the feelings and needs of others, which strongly implies that they did not receive enough nurturing to be capable of intimacy. While their physical needs might have been satisfied, something was missing on the deeper personal level. When asked about their childhood experiences, many adult narcissists will claim that they had a full measure of love and nurturing, dismissing the notion that they may somehow be deficient. Yet the chronic inability to truly enter another's world indicates otherwise.

I met Dale because his employer was on the verge of firing him. His repeated angry outbursts with co-workers and customers were a problem for everyone, so his employer insisted that he come to see me. Up to this point, Dale had kept his job, despite his surly reputation, because he was otherwise very bright and productive. As we talked in our initial session, it became quite obvious that Dale had little interest in learning about the people he encountered each day. He was self-assured to the point of arrogance, and he made it clear that he would have little conflict or anger if others could just learn to act right, by which he meant, "Do it my way."

In that first interview, as I asked him to describe his family history, he painted a picture of an ideal Norman Rockwell family. He described his mother as a caring person who was always available and who ran their household with great efficiency. She was an excellent cook, made sure Dale and his sisters went to parochial schools, drove him to sports activities, and helped with his homework. He described his dad as more quiet and driven to do well at his job, yet also friendly and loving. "If you're clamoring to find ugly skeletons in my closet," he said to me, "you're going to be very disappointed because I had a great childhood."

While I didn't argue with him, I grew more concerned about the accuracy of his report as I heard one story after another about his conflicts with people who did not meet his approval. He was a very critical man, though he only acknowledged that he had high standards. He was often defensive and rigid, and he could get angry if anyone suggested that he should change, dismissing their responses by saying, "They don't know what they're talking about." He exuded an air of superiority and liked receiving favored treatment, and he seemed to be on a never-ending quest to control his surroundings. The more I learned of him, the more clearly it seemed that he displayed strong narcissistic tendencies. My suspicions were confirmed when I saw that he rejected everything I tried to tell him. Every time I tried to tap into a subject that we needed to examine, he shut down the discussion with an airtight explanation that exonerated him from any fault or deficiency.

As our discussions continued, I began realizing that his idealized descriptions of his early family bonds were indeed exaggerated. Yes, his mother had been quite accommodating and lovingly available during his formative years, but their relationship was not anchored in deep emotional connections. Rather than being a parent who talked about relationship skills or about handling feelings such as anger or insecurity, she was simply a doting enabler who did his bidding and steered clear of emotionally challenging subjects. Rarely did she hold him accountable for his angry outbursts or restrain his feelings of entitlement. When she did discipline him, rather than making the situation an opportunity to teach Dale important life lessons, she simply corrected him, leaving him with the impression that he did not have to cooperate with those around him. While Dale's mother was physically available, they did not engage emotionally. Rather than being a parent who challenged Dale to explore the reasons for his emotions, she had a habit of excusing his rude behavior by agreeing that his childhood conflicts were the other person's fault. What Dale described to me as intimacy was not really intimacy at all. His external, physical needs had been well met, but he never learned to understand how relationships consist of complex skills that require care and understanding toward others.

Intimacy grows from experiences that allow us to explore the deeper aspects of our relationships. Beginning in the early years and extending into the teens, emotions need to be named. Children, for example, need to be taught to talk about their frustrations and to recognize what makes others feel frustrated. They need to talk about the reasons for their hurts and develop the ability to listen to others as they talk about theirs. Personal characteristics such as kindness and cooperation need to be discussed, so that the developing child can develop a sense of community with others. The absence of connections that foster these deeper personal explorations can keep children from gaining the ability to understand their own emotions or others'. As such children grow up, they ignore the reality of others' feelings and perspectives as they continually yield to their sin-produced impulses to satisfy only their own needs.

### A Fragile Sense of Self-Worth

While most narcissists tend to present themselves as having it all together, inwardly they operate like a little boy or girl who yearns to be greatly admired and frequently validated. They seek out others who will affirm their achievements, talents, or beauty, but it seems as though they can never get enough positive reinforcement. They are always hungry for more.

In normal development, children learn from their parents that they possess an inherent worth that is not attached to performance, looks, or status. That worth simply is. When the parent-child bonding is well established, and the child feels safe in the intimacy of the family, parents can reinforce the notion that despite mistakes or differences, the child can rest in the certainty that personal value is not a commodity that comes and goes; rather, it is a constant. For instance, if a child is angry at a playmate, the parent can say, "I know you're feeling disrespected right now, but let's talk about how you can hold onto your worth even when someone else rejects you." Or if a child loses a contest or earns an unsatisfactory grade at school, the parent might tell her, "I'd like you to do your best, but we still love and appreciate you, even when you don't come out on top." Parents and other adults have hundreds of opportunities to validate a child's worth by teaching that love and acceptance are completely separate from performance or popularity. External criteria can be put into proper perspective if the inner qualities are emphasized, but that, sadly, is not what budding narcissists learn.

Remember the story in Chapter One of how Jeff's sister Lana had a history of manipulating him and others? In addition to feigning cooperation so she could then demand favored treatment, she was known for talking behind others' backs in order to get what she wanted. Likewise, she was often secretive when she felt that openness might impair her chances to be in control. It was very important to her that she be treated as someone special.

In her childhood, Jeff told me, Lana seemed especially close to her mother. They had similar ideas about the need to get ahead by looking cute, having the right friends, and making good grades at school. Lana's mother was very opinionated and judgmental, so the closeness she shared with Lana was anchored in their strong convictions about the way life should be. They were bonded not so much by emotional ties as by their judgmental opinions.

Because Lana's childhood was filled with such a strong emphasis on being correct, it became important to her that she not display her weaknesses to anyone. Keeping a spotless image consumed much of her energies as she tried to demonstrate that she possessed correct knowledge and that she was above people who seemed weak or needy. Lana rarely admitted mistakes, and when she did, it was predictably someone else's fault.

Secure, confident, emotionally healthy people willingly and openly acknowledge that they have deficiencies and can make mistakes. They don't feel a need to portray themselves as ideal and can talk freely and specifically about their frailties even as they resolve to do better. Lana, however, was unable to be so authentic. Because opinions and judgments were such a central feature in her child-hood development, she had learned that the way to be secure was to be irrefutably right. This training actually sabotaged her sense of true worth. There was no room for any admission of hurt or need or weakness because that might imply inferior knowledge.

In a paradox that I have often noticed, strong people can admit their weaknesses, while weak people must appear strong. Narcissists, with a deep history of needing to look right and think correctly, show their fragility when they insist upon being seen as the ones who are above the problems of common individuals. Some, like Lana, have learned to fall back upon false smugness, while others were so aware of the unrelenting, omnipresent judgment that they are overcome with anxiety and shame. Either way, their focus on themselves became so dominant that it kept them from learning how to negotiate feelings other than their own.

### A Lack of Appropriate Submission

Narcissists come from every kind of upbringing, so it's impossible to say that they all have similar background experiences. But we can say that, in a variety of reasons and ways, they developed expecta-tions that the world owes them whatever they need. "What will you do for me next?" became a stronger and stronger theme as they ma-tured. This sense of entitlement can be fostered in either a highly privileged, solicitous family or in one where children are left to fend for themselves. In the first, children receive excessively favored treatment. They do not learn the value of sharing with or deferring to others because they are allowed to believe that they don't have to follow the same standards that others do. As a small illustration, most children are taught to respect cleanliness and order. Budding narcissistic children, however, might be excused from common drudgery such as household chores, even the ones directly affecting the child's immediate surroundings. "I'll do it for you," parents say. Or, in another example, when other adults (such as teachers and coaches) discipline a child, the child might balk. Parents who then excuse the child instead of requiring obedience convey the message that the child is above anyone else's authority. As these types of experiences add up, the child learns that submission to broader goals or general principles of goodness is not fully legitimate or necessary. Many adult narcissists have a history of parents who enabled them to ignore the need to be accountable or to follow the rules that were standard for their peers. The result is an adult life typified by a general unwillingness to cooperate with others as an equal.

In the neglectful family background that leads to a sense of entitlement, children are not spoiled as a prince or princess but are left to fend for themselves with very little adult input or supervision. With their raw, inborn self-centeredness intact, and with no one teaching them to curb their desires, these children develop a "why not?" mentality. "Why not go for all I can get," they learn to reason, "because no one else is going to take care of me." Their lack of deep attachments to their primary caregivers and their preoccupation with their own yearnings and needs can greatly inhibit their ability to cooperate with others or to account for others' feelings and needs.

In my experience, the most common evidence of a narcissist's exaggerated sense of entitlement is irrational anger when others do not go along with demands. Adult narcissists, for instance, can be truly shocked when others criticize their behaviors or motives. They think, "You would dare find fault in me?" Likewise, they struggle with experiences of defeat, turning their rage onto their supposed antagonist as they seek desperately to punish anyone who does not treat them royally. Their behavior and emotions illustrate how thoroughly they have failed to learn that life consists of both highs and lows, of favorable and unfavorable conditions.

Martin, Cindy's almost ex-husband, had a childhood history that had traces of both patterns. His parents divorced when he was in grade school, and he lived most of the time with his mother. An emotionally fragile and weak woman, she never seemed to know how to discipline Martin or how to teach him to consider her needs or those of his friends. With his strong-willed personality, he ruled the roost from an early age, and his mother was more than willing to play the role of maid and cook. He contributed only slightly to the upkeep of the house; when he was a teen, he established his own social guidelines, which were predictably quite loose. When he misbehaved, his mother rarely held him accountable. She clearly enabled his belief that his will was more valuable than anyone else's. For instance, if a relative drew attention to his selfish behavior, she would predictably say something like, "Oh he's just a lively boy who wants to have a little fun. Just leave him alone, he's harmless." She wouldn't discipline him because she didn't want to hurt his feelings.

Throughout Martin's childhood, his father lived nearby, yet they did not connect very often. Occasionally they would go hunting together, and as Martin grew older, he might spend the night at his father's place after a night of wild partying. His relationship with his dad could best be described as convenient, in the sense that they got together when it suited either of their short-term plans. They virtually never spoke about anything personal, and during visits, his dad would often hibernate in his bedroom with his two best friends: TV and Budweiser. Martin thought nothing of coming and going at his own whim, often not even communicating his whereabouts. Children must develop an appropriate appreciation for submission because it teaches them to consider the needs and feelings of others. Children who, like Martin, do not learn to factor in the needs of others at an early age predictably will be calloused to others' feelings in their later years.

## Exposure to Shame Games

The strong craving for control in narcissists typically grows out of a disordered sense of power dynamics. In their childhoods, usually one or both parents were overbearing or heavy-handed in dealing with anyone who dared to disagree with them. As children watch this behavior, they learn that others have to be forced into cooperation. Suppose, for instance, that a child's friend has been unfair in handling a conflict and now feels hurt and rejected. When the child tells his mother, she has a natural opportunity to help the child identify his emotions and learn to manage the strain in the friendship. For example, she might discuss his options for handling his angry feelings. Instead, the mother launches into a tirade about how inappropriate the friend is and calls the friend's parents and scolds them for raising such an insensitive child. She makes no efforts to take a balanced view of the situation, nor does she explore the circumstances of the conflict. Instead, she sees the situation as an offense that calls for confrontation—period. A child who witnesses these control tactics learns that he who gripes the loudest wins.

In another common scenario, a child might disobey or act in ways that simply displease her father. Dad could use the situation to explore the differences between his expectations and his daughter's, and the net result could be a greater understanding between them. Certainly they could talk about expectations about appropriate behavior, with the father listening respectfully to the child and the child doing the same. A parent with a disordered sense of power, however, could use the situation as an opportunity to show the child who is boss. He states his expectations in an overbearing manner and does not allow the child to respond. In the midst of such an exchange, the message the father is sending is, "I'm in charge around here, and don't you forget it." As the child feels shamed, she becomes confused. In the meantime, the opportunity is lost to teach the young girl how to interact successfully with people of different feelings and expectations.

When children witness such disordered displays of power from parents and key authority figures, they learn that while dominance might generate tensions in relationships, the strong-willed person eventually comes out ahead. They then can conclude that they need to imitate that kind of dominance if they want to maintain a competitive edge in this world. They learn to cling stubbornly to their positions, to criticize others before they are criticized, and to attack before attacked, all because they believe that such behavior creates a commanding aura that others cannot ignore—and that gets them what they want.

When they reach adulthood, people who have been exposed to years of power and shame tactics have lost any capacity to handle interpersonal tensions with objectivity. They certainly are not motivated to explore emotions with fair-mindedness. Rather than managing conflicts in ways that allow deeper understanding to develop in the relationship, they see conflicts as an immediate invitation to use their power. They never learned to listen, but they are very skilled at using blame and abruptness as tactics to help them take command.

Before Martin's parents divorced, his dad had a strong tendency to bully his mother. She had never developed the ability to be assertive, so she was often weak and confused in her responses. Martin's father capitalized on her insecurities whenever they argued by dredging up past mistakes, shaming her, and stubbornly refusing to change his mind even when he was clearly wrong. Martin witnessed his dad's displays of temper on many occasions as a boy. While he did not like the way they made him feel, he was quietly making mental notes about the ways to treat someone who had different opinions or preferences. His dad never said, "Son, here is the way you can pound an adversary into submission," but he did not have to. His actions showed young Martin that harsh and overpowering actions got results, and Martin used the same tactics when he grew to adulthood.

Narcissists vary in the ways they use to dominate and control. Some will be quite loud and forceful, while others use the silent treatment, and still others punish those around them through passive-aggressive behaviors such as refusing to cooperate or holding on to secrets. Some learn to overpower others through the use of tears to slyly elicit guilt in their adversaries. Still others might impose their perfectionist standards upon those they wish to dominate. Whatever the tactic, these narcissists have concluded that others should comply with their wishes, and they will not cease their overbearing ways until they have succeeded in proving their superiority.

## Mixed Messages About Right and Wrong

For narcissists, everything is relative. Their behaviors, beliefs, and priorities do not necessarily reflect what they really think, because they are responding only to what is happening in the moment, including their own feelings and needs. Narcissists often present themselves one way in one situation, then act entirely differently in another situation. A man, for example, might go to church and say all the right things to indicate that he is a deeply spiritual and religious person, then two days later go to a local bar's happy hour and not only get drunk but make lewd comments to the women there. Or a woman might behave in a friendly manner toward her child's teacher, praising her giftedness as they discuss the child's scholastic reports, yet the next day stride into the principal's office and berate the teacher for being inept. Because narcissists want their surroundings to make them feel comfortable, their standards for their own behavior can shift depending on the situation.

Commonly, this lack of consistency in matters of morality (the ability to discern right from wrong and act accordingly) has its roots in a childhood where a boy or girl witnessed discrepancies in the way key adults acted on their personal values. For instance, recall that Dale, who we met at the beginning of this chapter—the man prone to angry outbursts with his co-workers—painted a picture in my office of a highly moral, God-fearing home life that was presumably free from problems and pain. His father was a prominent member of the neighborhood church, and his mother had taught confirmation classes for years. They projected a squeaky clean image to the community, but Dale saw contradictions in their behavior. As a teenager, he once saw his father in a car with another woman, and his intuition told him this was not a business engagement. He later asked his dad about who the woman was and was quickly brushed off with a curt reply like, "That's not something we need to discuss."

When Dale saw his mother being very friendly with the senior minister's wife, he presumed they were close friends. But then he overheard telephone conversations in which his mother laughingly mocked the minister's wife, referring to her as "a clueless airhead." He told me that he recalled feeling confused by the difference between how she behaved in public and what she said in private.

Dale's early experiences were characteristic of other narcissists who often have a history of mixed messages in matters of truth and morality. Sometimes the lack of moral standards was so blatant that there was virtually no guidance at all about matters of right and wrong. More commonly, however, children such as Dale witnessed how their authority figures could behave completely differently in public from the way they behaved in private. In a few rare cases, I have seen that it was not so much blatant inconsistency but standards of goodness that seemed so far out of reach that the developing child quit trying to make the mark, reasoning that he or she could never measure up.

As children feel confused and conflicted about how they are supposed to conform to moral standards, they learn to read situations for clues as to how they should act in order to meet their immediate purposes most expediently. If compliance will get them what they want, they will feign a cooperative spirit. If they think lying is necessary, they will say whatever needs to be said. If it seems profitable to keep secrets or to reveal only partial truths, they will do that.

As adults, this kind of moral relativity causes narcissists to rationalize their tendency to allow their behavior to flow with the prevailing currents. That is why their reports about themselves cannot be fully trusted, and their allegiances can be fickle. They are loyal only to themselves; if they have to mislead others in the quest to get what they want, or if they contradict values they have said they hold, so be it. To them, truth is an expedient commodity in the pursuit of self-gratification.

## How Can You Respond?

In any interaction with a narcissist, it is inevitable they will lay the blame for any relationship breakdown at your feet. Since they can't incorporate insight at any deep level, the narcissist will fault you for his or her failings, and you might be tempted to think (falsely) that you are in fact responsible for the problem. When you start to think, "Where did I go wrong?" don't dwell on that thought. While it is always wise to listen to what others say, remember that narcissistic misbehavior is not a commentary on your worth. Rather, that misbehavior reveals a deep history of imbalances and inappropriate lessons learned from influential people in that person's past. The lack of awareness and tendency to blame you are merely indications that the narcissist's ego is too fragile to allow incisive self-examination.

With that in mind, you can respond to narcissistic behavior in the following ways.

### Respond with Your Mind, Not Your Emotions

In the case of Dale, who had been sent to counseling because of a problem with chronic anger and criticism of co-workers, I learned that more than one employee had been reduced to tears by his outbursts. His co-workers often huddled together, asking, "Why does he talk to me like that?" If they tried to confront Dale about his behavior, he dismissed them with rebuttals and rationalization, which was predictable because his upbringing had given him such poor insight into his behaviors. As a result, his co-workers were confused about how to proceed.

When I speak with people who are trying to deal with someone like Dale, I explain, "You can't afford to get emotionally drawn in by that person's barbs. Sad but true, this person will act in the same manner whether it is you or someone else in your same place. His behavior is not about you; it's about him. Always try to remember that you're just a player who happens to be on his stage." Someone like Dale is an inwardly tormented soul whose pessimism has caused him to conclude that the world is full of losers who get in the way of his own idealistic dreams. Such thinking is indicative of a long-standing dysfunctional defense system enlisted to preserve his ego at the expense of logic, common sense, or external evidence. Such a person has never learned healthy coping skills.

If you respond emotionally to narcissistic behavior, you are apt to lose sight of the truth about that person's error-filled past. Keep in mind that he or she has learned many improper life lessons; that insensitivity toward you is merely a reflection of that person's weak character development. While it is certainly normal to feel angry, frustrated, or disillusioned, it is best to take a deep breath and over-ride your emotional responses. You do not have to look to such a troubled person for validation of your own worth. The narcissist (no matter how powerful he or she seems) is not at all equipped to offer definitive opinions about your legitimacy, so you can give yourself permission to ignore any derisive pronouncements. Your beliefs about who you are can remain separate and untouched by that person's opinions or comments. Let your logic remind your emotions that you have goodness or decency even when the narcissist says or implies otherwise.

### Reflect on Your Own Past Imperfections

As I spoke with Cindy about her struggles in her marriage with Martin, she could see how his history of flawed and failed relationships had led him to respond to her in his self-absorbed way. "It is good," I told her, "to be aware that he had problems long before you showed up on the scene. Ultimately, you are not required to take responsibility for all the problems he falsely blamed on you. That said, as you learn what went wrong in his life, it would also be good for you simultaneously to take an honest inventory of your own history and the effects it has on your life now."

Cindy learned to examine her many emotional responses to Martin in a very objective manner. Knowing how strongly she had disliked his tendency to blame and accuse, she determined that if she was ever going to heal, she could only do so as she chose not to play the same games she had witnessed in him. She chose to look into herself in ways Martin never would.

Observing someone else's problems can prompt you to become honest about your own tendencies in the same direction. Knowing that we each have a self-absorbed child inside us, it is good to examine our emotions and behaviors routinely and see if we can detect selfishness. For example, we are likely to feel angry when we engage with a narcissist. That emotion is normal, but we can ask ourselves, "When I become angry, am I being responsible as I stand up for myself, or am I responding to an insult with an insult?" Likewise, as we witness how a narcissist can twist truth to fit his or her own biases, we might ponder, "Are my words consistently reliable, or do I too say whatever is necessary to promote my own selfish agenda?"

None of us is so pure that we are beyond the need for regular soul-searching. Though it can be very tempting to point a finger at a narcissist and ask, "What in the world is wrong with that person?" that accusing response fosters, however unintentionally, a spirit of bitterness. When we allow this to occur, the narcissist wins.

Cindy told me that one of the ongoing problems she had in her marriage to Martin was chronic resentment. "He was very difficult, and our struggles occurred almost daily. I would constantly wonder why he had to be such a jerk. I was full of hurt and agitation, and as the years passed, I was less and less capable of hiding my pain. Finally a close friend pulled me aside and talked with me about how she had seen my pleasant nature fade. She told me that she was fully aware that I had a difficult relationship with Martin but that I could no longer afford to let him rob me of the joy that I used to have. It was then that I went into serious self-examination and admitted that I did not like what had been happening to me. I had been so focused on responding to Martin's manipulations that I had neglected my own emotional healthiness."

Learning as much as possible about the narcissistic antagonists in your life will yield the greatest benefits *if* you simultaneously look closely at who you are. It makes no sense to gain insight into that person's past if you continue to respond to wrongs with wrong. Your knowledge would be empty indeed. Remember the phrase, "There but for the grace of God go I." Knowing that each of us starts life as that little toddler who can be cute yet selfish to the core, we can take our cues from the narcissist, recognizing that the absence of honest self-appraisal can bring results that are abysmally disastrous.

In Chapters Three and Four we will explore the different forms that narcissism takes. Some are quite open in their displays of controlling and self-absorbed behavior, while others can be very passive and secretive. As you learn to discern how these people can confound your emotions and relationship goals, you can become poised to learn the skills that will help you best respond to them.

Part Two

# *Recognizing the Patterns*

## Chapter Three

# The Narcissist with an Insatiable Need for Control

Diane came to see me because she was experiencing debilitating anxiety and panic attacks for the first time in her life. Single and in her midtwenties, she was building a career in marketing and felt confident that she had the skills to achieve professional success. She had a pleasant, outgoing personality that served her well in making and keeping contacts both in the workplace and in her personal life. "My professional life and social life give me little to complain about," she told me. "My greatest challenge is in knowing what to do with my mother. I know she loves me and is generally well intended, but she is very intrusive and bossy, and she seems to forget that I'm an adult who can make my own decisions. She lives about twenty minutes away, which isn't nearly far enough. She expects me to filter my life through her, and I'm not willing to do that."

As we talked, I learned that her mother wanted to talk with her virtually every day, presumably in order to be supportive. Diane suspected, however, that she had a deeper agenda; her mother was very nosy about the details of her personal life and was quite free in giving unsolicited advice. Making matters worse, Diane's older sister, Abby, was in many ways like her mother. When Diane's mother wasn't trying to direct her, Abby would step in. Diane had many memories of teen years filled with loud arguments with both her sister and her mother, and she was determined not to return to the explosive episodes of tears and chronic anger that had characterized those times. She had learned that reasoning with her mother never produced good results, and she saw no evidence that things were any different now. As I got to know Diane, it became apparent that she needed to interact less with her mother and sister. She had an active social life, so she was rarely at a loss for things to do or people to spend time with. But the challenge for Diane was to be strong enough to avoid emotionally capitulating to her mother's coercive attempts whenever Diane acted independently. Since her mother always wanted to take charge, Diane's job was not to allow herself to be unnecessarily controlled, even if it meant that she would have to find a way to deal with her mother's illogical arguments and attempts to make her feel guilty.

## An Insatiable Need for Control

If, like Diane, the narcissist in your life has an insatiable need for control, it is helpful to identify their most common behaviors. It's unlikely that you can change them or the behavior, but if you've developed an objective awareness, you can respond appropriately. As we said in Chapter Two, your best defense is awareness, not futile attempts to change the narcissist's behavior.

Let's start by seeing whether you're dealing with a hypercontrolling narcissist. Look over the following statements and note the ones that would commonly apply to you:

There are people in my world who won't accept no for an answer, no matter what.

I have felt manipulated by someone who has to have his or her own way.

I often get defensive reactions to what I do or say, even when I am being reasonable.

Others seem to have an ongoing list of expectations for me.

I regularly receive advice I didn't ask for.

When I am helpful or kind, the other person still wants more or is not satisfied.

The other person makes me feel guilty for choices that I know are right.

I have had to endure irrational, angry outbursts for no apparent reason.

I find myself measuring my words carefully to try to counteract another person's attempts to coerce my agreement.

The other person expresses his or her opinions in an insistent, relentless way.

My independent preferences are interpreted as selfishness.

I feel dominated by another's overly strict principles, rules, and directives.

If six or more of these statements apply to you, you are probably dealing with a highly controlling person who creates a smothering atmosphere that leaves you feeling emotionally wrung out. If you do not learn to sidestep the controlling person's overbearing ways, you are going to be worn down by your own responses. Remember, the narcissist is impervious to change, so it is useless to try to search for strategies to get them to abandon their controlling behavior. The key to learning to sidestep their attempts to dominate you is to recognize their behavior for what it is and formulate constructive responses. Let's look more closely at five ingredients that are common to the narcissist with an insatiable need for control.

## No Agenda but Theirs

There is nothing inherently wrong with having strong beliefs or opinions about the ways life should unfold. If anything, a lack of well-conceived convictions could result in an unhappy and purposeless life. The problem with narcissists, then, is not that they have a personal agenda but that they refuse to recognize that others can and should be allowed to establish their own paths as well. So sure are they of the correctness of their own ideas that they can hardly tolerate anyone with separate notions. To them, it is much more important to be right than to try to understand another's wishes or point of view. The result of this mind-set is constant pressure to impose their will in a way that brooks no disagreement.

### Sheer Force of Will

When we say that someone has a strong or forceful personality, we mean that he or she has a commanding presence that causes others to pay attention to and defer to them. People who have solid leadership qualities, who exude goodness, who openly encourage others, or who stand out as spiritual giants all exhibit strength of character. When forceful people are deeply committed to consistently good traits, they can become an inspiration for those who could use them as role models. Narcissists who have a forceful personality, however, are not at all likely to inspire others toward goodness. Their expressions of strength tend to feel smothering and invalidating, as they stifle others' positive traits and seek to get their way. As they manipulate and try to exert complete control over those around them, most people react very negatively, with anger, resistance, and argument. The narcissist counters stubbornly with even more inflexibility and other efforts to control. The net result is that others are repelled, and the relationship suffers or is destroyed.

### The Guilt-and-Duty Trump Card

In healthy relationships, partners can talk with one another about coordinating plans or making changes in a reasonable way, without intruding on one another's preferences or desires. Narcissists, however, are not inclined to communicate respectfully or constructively. They just want their way, and a give-and-take attitude is too risky— they might not get what they want. Instead they use heavy-handed tactics to force others to agree with them. They pull out "trump card" words such as *ought, should, have to, had better,* or *supposed to.* They browbeat their opponents with their distorted sense of duty and obligation. If you've been on the receiving end of such a barrage, you know that you end up feeling guilty just because you don't agree.

### The Only One Who Knows Anything

In their interactions with others, it's typical for a hypercontrolling narcissist to imply or even say directly that they are the only ones who know what to do in any given situation. For instance, if Diane were to tell her mother what route she thought that they should take in driving to visit a relative, her mother would probably say something like, "Where did you come up with *that* idea?" When Diane protests and tries to explain her preference, her mother might respond by saying, "I don't think that will work; let me tell you a better way." Narcissists have little faith in others' ideas (or, put another way, in anyone else's ideas besides their own), so when someone has a different idea, they instinctively try to find what is wrong. It would never occur to them that they might learn something from someone else. They simply don't trust others. Everything they say and do communicates a very low regard for others' decision-making skills.

### The Wear-You-Down Method

If you ask those who are regularly exposed to hypercontrolling narcissists, they will tell you how weary they feel after spending time with them. When narcissists first sense that they might lose control of a situation, rather than easing up or backing off, they take any resistance as an invitation to push harder. They will not be satisfied until they have their way, and they make no apology for using force to get it. One method they use is simply to wear down their "opponents" by whatever means is necessary to ensure that their opinions will prevail. And it's a method that works. When confronted with their relentless pressure, people finally just throw up their hands in disgust and say something like, "Okay, okay, we'll do it your way. Just leave me alone." The narcissist is delighted, and thinks, "Ah, you've finally seen the superiority of my way."

## How Can You Respond?

In one of our sessions, Diane said, "I am absolutely amazed at how hungry my mother is for control. There is such an irrational element in her thinking, but you could never tell her so. When I speak with her about something as simple as what I ate for lunch, she's got to push an opinion on me. I don't dare talk with her about my social life because she has all sorts of ideas about who I should get to know and where I should spend my time. She's so bossy it's absurd!"

Another one of my clients, Jeanette, could echo Diane's frustrations in her difficulties with a hypercontrolling husband. She had married Robert when she was only nineteen, but now as a middle-aged woman she was outgrowing many of the immature traits that had caused her to be susceptible to his Machiavellian ways. She explained, "Wherever he is, his personality fills the room. At first he can seem friendly, but it doesn't take long for people to feel uncomfortable with his intensity. He is never wrong, and he has opinions about everything. He could argue with a tree stump! As the years have passed, I have felt less and less comfortable with him in public because he is so full of himself. He dominates every conversation and makes little effort to know the little things about others. Life is always about him."

Jeanette went on to explain that she was reviewing her own history of being a people-pleaser, and she disliked what she was discovering about herself. "I can look back on countless times when I've just gone along with Robert solely to keep him from getting mad," she said. "In the meantime, I've become a shell of myself as I have stuffed my real feelings. I can't keep this up if I want to be a whole person. My dilemma is in knowing how to become more true to myself without setting off a major explosion from him."

When I speak with people such as Jeanette and Diane, I explain that while it is good to be sensitive to others' feelings, that sensitivity may in fact be enabling toxic patterns in their relationships. At some point, they will have to act independently, outside the narcissist's control, even if means risking the other's disapproval or anger. They do not have to force themselves to remain under another person's control if it means being disloyal to the life mission given to them by God.

### Choose Freedom

In their quest for control and dominance, narcissists do not consider that each of us is free to make our own choices. When God conceived humanity, he placed free will—the capacity to make our own choices—at the very heart of our humanity. Each person, without exception, possesses a free will. Some use it responsibly, while others do not. Either way, all of us want to be able to express our free will fully; when that ability is thwarted, we become frustrated, unhappy, and angry. In healthy relationships, where partners allow one another the space to maintain their uniqueness as they seek to coordinate their lives, freedom is most likely to produce positive choices. Such relationships are free of verbal or physical coercion, intimidation, guilt, or deception. Partners are open, willing to listen, and flexible; they recognize that differences are good and allow each person to grow at his or her own pace. When they speak to each other, they use an even, well-modulated tone of voice.

It would be wonderful if all relationships were this healthy and open, but most hypercontrolling narcissists wouldn't agree. They are so overbearing that it's common for their partners to assume that if the relationship is going to survive, they will have to give up and let the narcissist run things. But it does not have to be that way. Jeanette told me, "There have been times in my past when I felt so exhausted by Robert's forcefulness that I just gave up on myself. I quit doing even the smallest things that might bring out his criticisms." She told me, for example, that more than once she let go of friendships with people who did not meet Robert's approval. She stopped being involved in church and civic activities because he would complain about the disruptions they caused in their schedule. She stopped buying Christmas and birthday gifts for extended family members, not because they could not afford them but because she hated listening to Robert's predictable griping about the gifts. "Finally, a simple but life-changing thought occurred to me," she explained. "I realized that Robert had appointed himself king—and he was wrong to do so! I was not his slave, yet every time I gave over my will to him, I was actively encouraging him to keep pushing his controlling ways on me. He was wrong to deny my freedom, but I was equally wrong to give up my freedoms so willingly."

Diane had a similar realization. "I feel foolish for not recognizing how reasonable it is for me to be my own free person. I guess I have been so indoctrinated with the idea of honoring my mother and father that I didn't give myself permission to use common sense when my mother became so clearly disrespectful toward me."

When I speak with people such as Diane and Jeanette, I emphasize that freedom is not only a right; it is a responsibility. To give up our personal freedoms to a hypercontroller is to believe that God made a mistake when he endowed each of us with a distinct identity and approach to life. That's irresponsible behavior. None of us ever becomes successful by living according to someone else's ideas of who we should be. Rather, true success lies in discovering and realizing our own mission.

Diane nodded her head in agreement but grimaced as she asked, "You and I can say that it is good for me to be my own person, but I don't think I'll ever get my mother to agree. If I were to tell her that I have a God-given privilege to be what I was created to be, I'm absolutely sure she would tell me that I still needed to listen to her and follow her guidance. How should I respond to that?" Diane was echoing the same skepticism most people have about a controlling narcissist's inability to incorporate ideas from outside herself—no matter how sensible.

It is not your job to get the narcissist in your life to think correctly. Nor do you need that person's approval to act on your own. Because narcissists tend to dismiss decisions other than their own, they will undoubtedly respond to any of your assertions with another attempt to dominate you. Even though you can't get him or her to think the way you would like, you can still make your own choices. If you don't, you'll be invalidating your very self.

Unlike Diane, who was coming to see that asserting her own freedom was a natural part of blossoming into adulthood, Jeanette was struggling with a different type of dilemma in freeing herself from her husband Robert's overbearing nature. She admitted to me that she needed to be truer to herself, but she did not want to pay the price of a divorce. "Once I began making my own decisions without filtering every last detail through him," she explained, "I realized that I was redefining my role as his wife. Though I wanted to continue supporting him, as I became freer in my choices, he got angrier and angrier. He became more insulting and even more manipulative—he would give me the silent treatment and even cut off my access to our money. When I decided to go back to work so I wouldn't have to beg for a few extra dollars to buy simple things like cosmetics or clothes, he definitely became unhappy."

Jeanette had concluded that while there was a high price to pay for being free, it was not as high as the price she had been paying for giving up her freedom. By succumbing for years to Robert's domination, she had become chronically depressed, socially withdrawn, and unassertive in key family relationships. She summed up her feelings. "Life with Robert is going to contain tensions one way or another, so that is just a fact I'll have to accept. By letting him believe that it is acceptable to treat me as though I have no free will, I was neglecting a fundamental principle of human worth. I'm still very willing to be cooperative and loving toward him, but I cannot do that if I'm acting like a mouse." She decided that while she still wanted to remain married, she had an obligation to be a healthy person, not a whipped puppy. She remained committed to traits such as cooperation and responsibility, realizing that if Robert was still displeased, she did not have to give in to him. She accepted that if he could love her as she made healthy changes in herself, the nature of their relationship might have to change significantly. As you contemplate how to respond to a hypercontrolling narcissist, keep in mind that some responses foster your integrity and freedom and some don't. In the sections that follow I outline the ones that don't work in your favor:

**1. Don't Cater to Them.** It is tempting in dealing with hypercontrolling narcissists to allow short-term considerations to overshadow long-term consequences. Most people such as Diane and Jeanette know that each time they go along with the controller for the sake of avoiding conflict, their misery will only increase. The narcissist is likely to feel empowered and think, "I knew I was right, and I'm glad you agree." It's easy to convince yourself that the path to peace requires an ultrasubmissive response, but that response costs you your freedom of choice.

For instance, Jeanette could recall many past scenarios when Robert overruled her decisions about how to discipline her teenage daughter. She sometimes argued for her decision but commonly stopped and went along with his mandates. She did not want to make the daughter feel trapped in the crossfire. Finally it dawned on Jeanette that her effectiveness as a parent was about to be lost completely. She admitted, "If I don't begin standing firmly in my decisions at home I'm going to prove that my status in the family is meaningless. What kind of role model would that be to my daughter?"

By catering to him, Jeanette had to put up with fewer and fewer haranguing lectures from Robert, but the long-term consequence was that she appeared to be a weak and disengaged mother. Jeanette began realizing for the first time in her marriage that she could choose whether to appease Robert or assert herself and her ideas.

**2. Don't Evade the Narcissist.** Another unproductive tactic for responding to hypercontrolling narcissists is to try to avoid or escape their abrasive and distasteful behavior. This is not always a wrong choice, especially when the relationship is either extremely abusive or superficial. Many people, for instance, disengage from a promising friendship when it becomes apparent that the friend proves too pushy or domineering to warrant trust. Such a decision could actually be wise. But in the case of more intimate relationships, especially with a parent or spouse, it might not be entirely possible or even wise to disconnect, although, it's tempting. For instance, Diane decided to spend less time with her mother than the mother wanted, and I agreed with her. There were times, however, when her desire to keep her distance proved awkward and unnatural. Once Diane was visiting with her sister, Abby, when their mother unexpectedly dropped by. Diane was so determined to avoid her mother that she left her sister's house abruptly. Later she explained to me that she felt so unimportant when her mother arrived that she preferred not to be there. She just didn't want to be open or honest with her mother about why she felt as she did. She rationalized her behavior by saying, "I just didn't want to get into it with her."

While it is understandable that Diane did not want to get into an unnecessary argument with her mother, it is also true that she did not need to let her visit with her sister be ruined by her mother's arrival. Running away actually gave her mother more power—and that led inevitably to even more troubled emotions.

**3. Stop Trying to Force Them to Quit Being Manipulative.** The old phrase "fight fire with fire" might seem like a good remedy for dealing with hypercontrolling narcissists, but it's not. When a narcissist hears that you disagree, the response is most likely to be forceful rebuttals in which he or she tries to force your agreement. You end up in a pointless exchange of accusations, attacks, and arguments. Jeanette described to me how her communication with Robert had become increasingly volatile once she decided not to succumb to his micromanagement of her life. Robert couldn't bear for Jeanette to set her own priorities; he stepped up his criticisms, causing Jeanette to try to explain even more forcefully how wrong he was in his treatment of her. It was futile, but Jeanette didn't see a way out.

I asked Jeanette, "When you beg and plead with Robert to stop being so controlling, how often does he say something like, 'Gee, Honey, I really appreciate the input. That really makes sense'?"

"Huh," she sneered. "You've got to be kidding. He wouldn't say that in a million years. If anything, he just responds to my assertions with greater force."

"If arguing hasn't changed his responses in the past, you might be deluded in thinking it will make a difference in the future," I replied. "I think your energies would be more successfully spent determining why you get caught in such an empty exchange."

When you attempt to change a chronic manipulator, you are probably engaging in a form of mythical thinking, which means that fantasy, not reality, is guiding your efforts. It can be a fantasy to assume that somehow your words will suddenly prompt the narcissist to change course and become empathetic and reasonable. Begging and pleading might seem like an option when you feel frustrated at the narcissist's behavior, but it ultimately does not work. There has to be another way.

## Responses That Work with Controllers

It might be disappointing to realize how very limited you are in your ability to get a hypercontrolling person to change. As this reality sets in, you face the prospect that the relationship will not be as satisfying as you would like it to be. But you can couple that realization with the awareness that you do have options in how you respond to that person. You can still choose to be healthy, even if the narcissist does not join you. There are four productive ways to respond to a hypercontrolling person that will allow you to retain your sanity, your integrity, and a greater sense of control over your own life.

**1. Choose Your Own Path.** Though the controlling narcissist in your life would have you believe otherwise, it is entirely reasonable to choose instead to go your own way rather than go along with him or her. The person will protest in no uncertain terms, but that does not need to dissuade you from your resolve to follow your own path. In this way you let loyalty to your own well-laid plans take priority over appeasement or defensiveness.

Jeanette was realizing that it was time to decide who would be in charge of her personal well-being. She had been filtering so much of her emotional stability through Robert's moods that she felt as if she had been on a long personal rollercoaster ride. She wanted a better way of life. When she and I spoke about taking a more proactive approach to her own destiny, she was definitely receptive, yet she wanted to know how her changed thinking would translate into real lifestyle differences.

I started off by saying, "First, let's pinpoint specific incidents when you hand over the direction of your emotions and behaviors to Robert." We listed quite a few common scenarios. For instance, she tended to buckle quickly when Robert criticized her parenting decisions. She either cried or withdrew when he insulted her tastes in decorating or selection of clothing. She became quickly defensive when he questioned how she set priorities in her work and home schedules.

As we reviewed how easily she had succumbed to fear, pouting, and empty arguing in dealing with Robert, I asked, "How do these responses fit into your overall plans for a productive life?"

Her response was direct. "They don't fit at all." I then asked if she could make a list of traits she would like to dominate her personality most of the time, and she had no difficulty articulating them. She mentioned how she would like to be known as confident, patient, honest, reliable, understanding, calm, and respectful. At that point I challenged her, "Would you be able to maintain these traits even when Robert is acting in his adversarial ways?" She knew that I was looking for a "yes" response, but she had to pause to consider if that scenario indeed was possible.

I explained further, "Jeanette, you are under no obligation to be defensive when Robert challenges your decisions. If you want, you can cry or appease, or if you want you can develop your separate plans and stick to them, without defending them at all." She looked at me, and I could see she was trying to imagine how she could possibly follow such a path with Robert. I went on, "Likewise, when he dictates how you should rearrange the way you handle a family matter, you don't have to drop your common sense and just go along with his mandates. Instead, you can resolve to hold firmly to your separate notions. That would display confidence in yourself."

Jeanette nodded slowly. "I know that Robert will go into his bully mode when I follow through on my own plans, and I become very tired of arguing my case with him."

My response was plain and simple. "Who says you're required to argue your case? It's possible for you to go your own path with or without his agreement or approval. You'll want to make sure that your motives are pure and you communicate your beliefs respectfully. At that point, Robert can decide how he wants to respond to you. It's not necessary for you to plead your case."

Often people like Jeanette tell themselves that their primary goal should be to gain the narcissist's cooperation and approval, but in doing so they forfeit their own personal initiative. But it doesn't have to be that way. She can determine instead to be specific in the ways she will manage each interaction with Robert, choosing the best way to behave regardless of what the narcissist thinks or wants. She can focus on trying to live in a healthy way rather than settling for the false peace of appeasement. If Robert responds in childish or bullying ways, Jeanette doesn't have to try to make Robert feel happy or go along just to keep the peace. To do so would only perpetuate her misery and dishonesty.

**2. Maintain Self-Respect.** Life with the narcissist's messages of invalidation and disregard can be like water dripping slowly on a rock, eroding your self-respect and self-esteem. As we've discussed, narcissists have a deep-seated sense of inferiority, but instead of admitting this and making necessary internal adjustments, they falsely compensate for those feelings by attempting to assert their superiority. As a part of their twisted logic, they believe that a way to appear strong is to diminish the value of those in their presence. Your job is to recognize this syndrome and choose not to be drawn into their false thinking.

We all deserve to be respected in our relationships—and that includes you. While it is unfortunate that narcissists don't comply with such a fundamental notion, you can choose to maintain your self-respect even in the face of their messages to the contrary.

In one of our sessions, I asked Jeanette, "If you were to display consistent respect for yourself, how would it be shown?" She paused for a moment, then replied, "The word that comes to my mind is *worth*. I would act as if I am a person of worth."

"You're implying that you allow yourself to be treated as a person of diminished worth. Is that right?"

Her reply was to the point. "As I've been examining how Robert has treated me over the years, I have concluded that he doesn't have any regard for my basic worth. But then, as I consider it more fully, I can see that I have not lived as one who values myself. I mean, there have been countless times when I have acted like someone whose opinions are empty. I've reneged on plans that I wanted to implement. I've taken insults without considering that they might be wrong. It's time for me to quit focusing so much on the things about Robert that bother me. I need to concentrate instead on the ways I add to my own miseries by invalidating myself." Her insights were impressive.

Our behaviors are ultimately a reflection of our deepest beliefs. When you persistently tolerate others' rude or intrusive behaviors, you are saying that you do not believe that you possess enough dignity to stand up for your needs or convictions. The irrefutable truth is that each of us has a God-given value that cannot be rescinded by the declarations of misguided humans. Somewhere along the way, you allowed a narcissistic human to become your final authority, not God. You can replace human judgment with your confidence in your intrinsic worth. Like Jeanette, you can admit the futility of allowing a hypercontrolling narcissist to declare your worth or lack of it. You can choose instead to take full ownership of your extraordinary value as a human being. When Jeanette really understood this point, she told me, "I am learning that each time I feel belittled by Robert, I can weigh his pronouncements against my own beliefs. If his opinions do not match what I know to be true, I'm under no obligation to build my day around them."

*3. Establish Boundaries and Consequences.* Every healthy relationship is anchored in a mutual regard for personal boundaries and limits. This means both parties openly acknowledge that they have distinct preferences and beliefs and that it is good to allow those distinctions to be displayed. In fact, in healthy relationships, boundaries are not only accepted, they are encouraged.

Because narcissists are so preoccupied with control and dominance, they are likely to step over personal boundary lines. That means it is up to you to establish the boundaries that the narcissist will not initiate. For instance, when Christmas came, Diane's mother expected her to spend four or five nights at her home, despite the fact that they only lived twenty minutes apart and that Diane did not want to stay at her mother's house. In times past, Diane would have argued loudly and tried to resist but would eventually relent and do what her mother wanted her to do. In one of her breakthroughs, Diane told me, "I've decided that arguing with my mother does no good because she is such a poor listener, and besides, not once have I succeeded in changing her thinking. This year, though, I'm taking a different tack when she insists that I spend several nights with her during the holidays. I'm going to let her know what my separate plans are, and if she cannot accept them, I'll just have to pull back. I'll spend time with the family both on Christmas Eve and the next day, but I'll spend the night at my own place. If she goes into her pouting mode, I'll cut my visit short and instead spend my time with people that I want to be with. I simply refuse to go along blindly with her drama." I agreed that if her mother could not be flexible, it was necessary for Diane to communicate through her behaviors that she was setting boundaries and that there would be consequences for abrasive treatment.

When Diane begins to establish boundaries and consequences in reaction to her mother's pushy behavior, her mother will probably say she's being selfish. Since no healthy person wants to behave in a selfish manner, it is important for Diane to understand the difference between selfishness and self-preservation. Selfish behavior is all about maintaining tight control over one's life, whereas self-preserving behavior allows us to take care of ourselves so that we can be more present to and more helpful to others. A self-preserving person *wants* to fit into others' plans, but with reasonable limits. Narcissist would never understand the difference, since their behavior is always selfish.

**4. Remove Yourself from the Person or Situation When Necessary.** It is never desirable to end a relationship, particularly when marriage or family ties are involved. Long-standing, ongoing relations with family members can enhance personal satisfaction, even when it becomes necessary to make room for negatives. That stated, those relationships need not be maintained at the cost of personal stability. When hypercontrollers become so overbearing that they destroy others' emotional well being, it can be reasonable to withdraw from the relationship altogether.

Neither Diane nor Jeanette determined that it was necessary to cut themselves off from the hypercontrollers in their lives. Jeanette, in particular, realized that if she made the decision to divorce, the repercussions would be too difficult for her and her daughter to bear. She did, however, explain to Robert that she would not continue to maintain the status quo if he became abusive or attempted to actively undermine her new choices to be her own person. "I told him that I would not allow him to take me for granted like I have done in the past. For years, he has just assumed that good ol' Jeanette would just hang around and tolerate his domineering, but I think he is beginning to see that I'm no longer taking on the role of his verbal punching bag."

Robert was not fully pleased with Jeanette's newfound freedom, but he did begin recognizing that he had pushed her beyond her limits of tolerance. As she showed more resolve to be healthy, he slowly began adjusting his responses to her. Jeanette was fortunate; many people who relate regularly with narcissists find that their efforts to be free are not met with such acceptance or acquiescence. If that's the case, they will be at a crossroads as they grapple with the question of what is best for the future. Some will decide that if maintaining ties with a narcissist includes problems with ongoing emotional disorders, they are wiser to choose personal stability over toxic relational ties. They correctly interpret their emotions of chronic anxiety and anger as signals that they are on overload and need relief.

As you make the necessary changes in your responses to a hypercontrolling narcissist, you will have mixed feelings. On the one hand, you might feel relief, even exhilaration, as you are truer to the real you. On the other hand, you may feel hurt and disappointed because the narcissist will not approve of your changes. It is sad but true that he or she will probably be perplexed at your efforts to act independently. In the end, however, you cannot afford to let that person's response dictate the strength of your resolve.

To make your journey with a narcissist even more complicated, you will need to factor in the possibility that he or she will shift gears, becoming passive-aggressive. We'll explore productive responses to that potential in Chapter Four.

## Chapter Four

# The Passive-Aggressive Narcissist

Barbara had just about reached the end of her rope. She just couldn't get her brother, Donald, to play a more active role in taking care of their ill and aging father. Both in their late forties, the two were only eighteen months apart in age and lived within a few miles of their dad, who was struggling with Parkinson's disease and other ailments. He wasn't quite ready to enter a full-care nursing facility, but he needed help getting to the grocery store and doctors' appointments. Though he could do simple kitchen tasks, he liked to have others take him out to cafes or bring him a home-cooked meal. Barbara had taken the lead in caring for her father and did her best to make herself available to help in his care, even enlisting the help of his elderly friends from church to drive him when he needed a ride. Even so, there were still times when Barbara needed Donald's help, but he just wasn't reliable when it was his turn to pitch in.

For one thing, Barbara told me, it was not uncommon for Donald to agree to take their father to a doctor's appointment, only to have her father call at the last minute to tell her that Donald had failed to pick him up. When she tried to call Donald, he didn't answer his cell phone. Or Donald might tell his father that he would spend an afternoon working in his garden, but then thirty minutes into the project would leave and not tell anyone where he was going. When Barbara tried to talk reasonably to Donald about his lack of reliability, he would apologize profusely and promise to do better. But he never did. He let Barbara and their father down time after time.

Donald's adult behavior was hardly different from his actions as a boy. Frumpy and unkempt, he had been the poster-boy for sloppiness, always late wherever he went. As a student he had accumulated many zeroes on school projects, not because of a lack of intelligence but because of a failure to turn in assignments. In fact, his only constant was his lack of reliability. It seemed that Donald did not want anyone else telling him what to do or when to do it, nor did he want or take any responsibility, but he didn't say so directly. He just didn't comply.

While it is easy to presume that the bottomless need for control manifests as bossiness toward others, it can take other forms as well. Sometimes narcissists disguise their self-absorption by appearing to be mellow and agreeable on the outside but are in fact refusing to engage openly or cooperate with others. This kind of person is aggressive but not directly so, as with a hypercontrolling narcissist, which is why we call their pattern *passive-aggressive*. They assert their will by being passive, by refusing to cooperate or comply with others' wishes. They may display many of the traits we discussed in Chapter Three but add the wicked twist of being more devious and less obvious in the way they retain control.

Because they resent any responsibilities imposed on them, passive-aggressive narcissists will do all kinds of unpleasant things to avoid personal accountability. They are stubbornly unreliable, often lazy, and hard to teach. Even if you can get them to seem to comply with your requests, you'll only get indifference and broken promises. Trying to force change in a passive-aggressive person is frustrating, and success is rare indeed.

To get a more complete idea of the way a passive-aggressive narcissist behaves, consider the following list of common traits:

- Being deliberately evasive
- Giving the silent treatment as a means of expressing disapproval
- Procrastinating or being lazy
- Giving half-hearted efforts

- Promising to do something, then not doing it
- Saying what another person wants to hear, then acting contrarily to what was said
- Deliberately avoiding knowledge of another person's needs or difficulties
- Giving the appearance of friendliness, but not behaving as a friend
- Being secretive or doing things out of others' view
- Employing timing (too late or early) that frustrates or undermines others
- Being sloppy and disorganized
- Regularly portraying a careless attitude
- Complaining behind other people's backs, but refusing to discuss problems openly

One of the most frustrating elements in the passive-aggressive pattern is that it is a pattern, not just a single instance. It's very difficult to get this kind of person to be honest about the meaning of their selfish behavior. For instance, if you talk with a passive-aggressive person about being late in completing a project, you will hear something like: "I really meant to be finished by now, but a major emergency came up that I had to tend to." Or if you draw attention to the disorganization in that person's office or home, you might hear something like: "I was planning to get everything in shape, but I came down with a sinus headache." They seldom respond with an honest acknowledgment of their shortcomings. Someone who is simply a procrastinator and who is explaining why a project has not been started would say, "It bothered me when you asked me to take on the assignment, so I guess I've been taking out my feelings on you by not getting started on it." Such forthrightness is highly unlikely from a passive-aggressive narcissist. You can try to talk openly and honestly with such a person, but they'll keep evading you. The net result is likely to be frustration.

## Understanding the Pattern

One of the best ways to manage the passive-aggressive narcissists in your life is to understand the different components of the pattern. Once you do, you can manage your own frustration and figure out more effective ways to respond to them.

### Hidden Anger

Passive-aggressive narcissists are full of anger—not the loud, harsh words or ranting and raving that we normally associate with anger, but a whole other manifestation. Passive-aggressive people are masters at acting out their anger without appearing agitated. They have observed that others make fools of themselves when they are explosive, and they certainly don't want to do that. They have also learned that anger can actually be more effective (in helping them maintain control) when it is expressed more slyly. For instance, Donald's disappearance after completing only a small portion of the yard work for his dad was his way of conveying anger at being asked to do it in the first place. Likewise, his habit of chronic lateness indirectly communicates his feelings: "Look, I do things in my own timing, and I don't need anyone telling me how to run my life; the sooner you figure this out, the better off we will all be!"

Anger in itself is not something to be avoided at all costs. Justified anger can prompt individuals to take a stand for beliefs that are right and good. It is an emotion of self-preservation when it is a response to non-cooperation, rejection, insensitivity, invalidation, criticism, and the like. In its most appropriate forms, anger can be linked to the drive for personal respect. It can prompt individuals to ask that their legitimate needs be considered and to hold to their convictions. In healthy relationships, partners make room for conflicts and differences, and they can agree to express anger with respect and self-restraint.

Narcissists can experience anger just like anyone else, but because they are so focused on themselves, they look for ways to express it that will satisfy personal needs even if it disrupts others' needs. That kind of anger is aggressive without necessarily being direct. Narcissists are most interested in their own self-preservation and in manipulating other people to get what they want. Passive-aggressive narcissists manipulate quietly but very persistently; they don't appear overtly angry most of the time but do act out their anger in less direct ways. If you ask them whether there is frustration or anger behind their uncooperative behavior, they'll deny it over and over. But the anger behind their messages of noncompliance comes through loud and clear.

### Secret Fears

In healthy interactions and relationships, people exchange feelings, preferences, and ideas openly and allow themselves to know and be known fully. They realize that feeling connected is a by-product of the authenticity they are nurturing by their openness and honesty.

Passive-aggressive people have not developed enough trust in others to be truly open. In fact, they shun opportunities to reveal who they really are because they feel that there is too much risk that they will lose power if they reveal themselves. If you press them to explain why they don't want to be more open, they are likely to place the blame outside themselves, saying that others would not respond to them fairly. This reaction actually masks a greater problem of lack of trust in their own ability to manage conflicts successfully. For instance, Donald knew that if he owned up to his evasiveness, his sister could easily expose his selfishness, and he feared that he might not win the debate with her. His silence reflected his knowledge that he really couldn't justify his behaviors.

Passive-aggressive people can recall historical events where significant others acted in less than honorable ways. Perhaps they remember how a parent was too brash or forceful in responding to disputes. Some might have had bullying siblings or extended family members who made life miserable for them. They might have been exposed to peer groups who were not kind and accepting.

Whereas healthy people can learn to manage such common frustrations, passive-aggressive narcissists remain preoccupied with the potential for being mistreated. These possibilities, and similar other distressful experiences, have caused them to conclude that the world is a hostile and fearful place, and the only way to survive is to keep up a solid wall of protection. This is what is behind behaviors such as evasiveness, withdrawal, and rationalization. Because they are afraid, passive-aggressive narcissists have lost the ability to see these past experiences objectively. They are so busy accusing others of having mistreated them that they overlook the truth that they still can learn to incorporate realistic beliefs about their inner strength that can counterbalance external threats.

For instance, a man who was once exposed to rejecting family members can incorporate the notion that those antagonists were misguided and that he is no longer required to sift his adult beliefs through their wrong pronouncements. He can choose to define himself and trust in his own reasoning. Unfortunately, many passive-aggressive adults never learn to truly challenge what (and who) was wrong in their past experiences. They remain stuck in fear because their history did not allow them to develop confidence in problem-solving interactions. As they allow fear to develop ever-deepening roots, they extend it into pessimistic notions about life, and this pessimism allows them to feel justified in keeping others at arm's length.

Donald, for example, often spoke about how he did not like to talk openly with his dad about personal plans or preferences. Indeed, his father had a history of being so opinionated and pushy and demanding, that from a very early age Donald was afraid to share thoughts or feelings that might arouse his father's ire. He developed a habit of saying whatever was necessary to appease his father, even when he knew that it didn't reflect what he really intended to do. As an adult, he continued to be guarded in his father's presence; he still did not feel comfortable being himself. As he had grown into late adolescence and early adulthood, he had never learned to challenge the notion that it was not safe to respond to his dad's overbearing ways by being upfront with his feelings and actions. Instead, he was deeply angry at having to continue to appease his father and hide his true feelings. Donald's fear was in direct proportion to his lack of trust in the legitimacy of his own decisions, and he displayed that fear each time he chose to be less than open with his real feelings and ideas.

You can see a narcissist's fear in the defensiveness that is so common in his or her personal exchanges. In offering rationalizations for their behavior, seeming excessively cautious, making excuses, getting very angry over little things, and seeming generally unwilling to talk about personal matters, they are showing their belief that being genuine is too risky. This belies an assumption that if they disclose who they really are, they will be injured or criticized in some way, something they want to avoid at all costs. Their defensiveness might also manifest as strident efforts to justify their own notions while simultaneously denouncing others' thoughts and feelings. Or they simply withdraw or choose not to participate in activities that might require them to express their real thoughts. In any case, their fear of disclosing who they are and what they feel leads them to adopt an adversarial stance in their relations with others.

Barbara told me that she had once attempted to talk to Donald about his reluctance to participate constructively in managing family problems. When she mentioned that she wanted to determine how they could be more considerate of each other's needs, he quickly shot back, "There you go trying to tell me how to prioritize my life." She assured him that she was only attempting to open the lines of communication, but he once again blurted out, "I'm not going to let you dictate to me what I should and shouldn't do."

As she reflected on the exchange during one of our sessions, she said, "As I think about it, Donald has been defensive with me for years. I can barely get a thought out of my mouth before he assumes that I have some sort of negative motive. Once he makes up his mind that I'm out to get him, he then feels justified in hiding out somewhere. I swear he is the most elusive man I've ever known."

While Donald would never say it explicitly, his passive-aggressive behavior indicated his real thoughts: "I'm feeling threatened right now, and I'll need to protect my personal interests by going underground."

## Lack of Accountability

Psychologically healthy people know that relationships require openness, give and take, and accountability to one another. They understand that openness is a vital component of teamwork and welcome the chance to know others and to be known. Every relationship requires cooperation, if it is to be satisfactory, and a sense of fair play prompts mutual appreciation of the need to direct and to submit, depending on the situation. But for passive-aggressive narcissists, this kind of balanced give and take is threatening. They feel as though they are losing control—and that's the last thing they can stand to do. Their high need for control leads them to evade the normal obligations of their relationships; being cagey and wily and slipping away keeps others from imposing their preferences. Because they assume the worst, they cannot conceive that others might not actually want to control them. That's why they often refuse accountability; if they're being held to a promise or obligation, it means they have to consider someone else's ideas or priorities. And they don't want to do that, either.

Donald had many more problematic relationships than just the one with his sister, Barbara. His marriage fell apart, and he divorced in part because of his use of money. Specifically, he refused to let his former wife know how much money he earned. He was self-employed, so his paychecks varied from month to month, but he gave her the same amount each month and didn't divulge how much more (or less) he had earned. When Donald's wife filed divorce papers, she tried to discover how he had managed his bank accounts, but he had apparently kept his extra money in cash, leaving no paper trail. She was certain he had stashed large sums away but could offer no proof, and ultimately she was unable to get the settlement she had wanted.

Barbara commented to me, "Donald's secretiveness about money is just par for the course. There are times when he'll disappear for the weekend, telling no one where he is. I suspect he goes away for gambling trips at his favorite casinos, but he'll never say a word about his whereabouts. I'm sure he drove his poor wife crazy because he never liked anyone knowing his business."

Relationships do require that we give up some control in order to be accountable, but healthy people know this is not the same as being deprived of power or autonomy. With accountability comes relationship security and clean communication, ingredients that enhance anyone's quality of life. Passive-aggressive people, however, are often "lone wolves" who are so consumed with maintaining power that they forego relationship security and communication. In their minds, when no one knows what is happening in their personal lives, they are better off.

## How Can You Respond?

If you have spent much time around passive-aggressive narcissists, you can probably relate to the analogy of walking through a minefield. Experience tells you to be on guard, since their reactions are unpredictable. The possibility of sudden disappointments or unexpected conflict is so strong that it is very difficult to remain calm, cool, and collected. To avoid being drawn into their manipulative games, you will need to be vigilant.

One of the most common games to avoid could be called "Gotcha." An episode between Barbara and Donald will illustrate how this game works. While visiting at Donald's house, Barbara decided it would be a good time to discuss weekend plans involving their dad. When she asked about his schedule, Donald continued to putter around in the kitchen as if he did not hear her. Raising her voice, Barbara again mentioned that she needed to know his schedule so they could coordinate their father's care. Donald mumbled something, to which Barbara shouted loudly, "Look, I'm trying to get some input from you and I need you to talk to me. Tell me your plans for this weekend!" Blank-faced, Donald turned around and stared at her. "How do you expect me to make plans with you when you stand there yelling at me?" That said, he silently walked to another part of the house, refusing any further discussions. Gotcha!

In his passive, unresponsive way, Donald had baited his sister into speaking rudely, which then allowed him to point the accusing finger toward her. Forget that he didn't have the decency to answer her question directly; once she shouted at him, he seized on that, and it became the only thing that mattered. When she later tried to revisit the same issue of making weekend plans, he piously mentioned that he would like to cooperate but would no longer consider doing so because of her insulting behavior. In the meantime, in his eyes, he was perfectly innocent in the exchange.

As you cope with and manage your responses to a passive-aggressive narcissist, it very important that you not let that person draw you into toxic exchanges. You can rest assured that fairness will not be one of their operating principles, so you'll need to anticipate their responses and act accordingly. Let's examine several ideas that can keep you on track.

### Stand Firm

Passive-aggressive narcissists always want to weaken their partners' resolve. Their lack of cooperation sends a strong message that they have low regard for team spirit, and that attitude is not likely to abate. But that doesn't mean that you have to behave in the same way. While you cannot force passive-aggressive persons to cease being what they are, you can evaluate your behavior to determine whether (or how) you are contributing to an overall atmosphere of dysfunction.

For instance, you might notice that you openly argue with the narcissist about his or her controlling behavior, but in the process you are contributing to a contentious atmosphere—and that is not a good trend. You could choose instead to stop trying to persuade and confidently go about your business with or without their approval. By doing this, you set your own priorities, as opposed to worrying excessively about what the narcissist thinks. Commonly, people such as Barbara make the mistake of doubting themselves and their handling of interactions with passive-aggressive narcissists. So focused are they on the wrongs done to them that they slip into a victim's role that renders them ineffective and indecisive. For instance, when Donald behaved in a cool and dismissive way toward her, Barbara would often become hung up on the question, "What have I done to make him treat me so poorly?" She would fall into the trap of assuming that his irresponsibility was a commentary about her, and that would diminish her ability to see the situation clearly.

Narcissists want you to lose faith in yourself and your decisions because it makes it easier for them to move forward unencumbered by your wishes or feelings. Even though you are not likely to prevail against their scheming ways, you are not helpless, nor do you have to lay down your resolve. You can only be controlled if you allow yourself to be controlled. You can respond with firmness and confidence to their manipulation.

As Barbara and I talked about her relationship with Donald, I asked her to take an inventory of her behavior that she felt was contrary to her personal standards. After some reflection, she told me that she was too prone toward communicating coercively. She pleaded too strongly with him and analyzed his behavior to the extent that it became obsessive. She appeased him too readily. In short, she realized that she was so consumed with her brother's behavior that she had slipped into unproductive patterns of responding to him—patterns that were hurting her and not getting her the results she wanted from him.

I challenged Barbara to consider how she might conduct herself even when she knew he would not respond as she wanted him to. "The first word that comes to my mind is *decisive*," she said. "I need to remain decisive even when he is wishy-washy or worse." For example, Barbara admitted that even when she seemed to gain an agreement from Donald, she still doubted that he would follow through. She'd become tense and anxious thinking about how he was about to let her down. This could easily result in hours of silently fretting and fuming about his behavior. As an alternative, she decided that she could be much more direct with him about her expectations and clearly state the consequences if he didn't comply. If she sensed that he was not going to keep their agreements, she decided she would leave him alone and seek other ways to meet her needs. "I've spent too much time hanging in limbo wondering if Donald would do what he promised. Now, if I have any hint that he will fail me, I'm going to be much more willing to explore my other options. I've got too much on my mind to worry about what he will or will not do."

As you choose to stand firm in your reactions to a passive-aggressive narcissist, you'll want to avoid two extremes. First, you need not be so polite that you fail to speak directly and to the point. Let the person know your needs and expectations without equivocation. If you see that they're going to respond in an unproductive way, make plans without having to curry the narcissist's favor. Second, you don't need to be so blunt that you are rude. Firmness does not mean disrespect. You can use a tone of voice that is dignified even as it is also determined.

### Keep Your Expectations Low

Passive-aggressive narcissists are not likely to change. If you hold out high hopes for getting their cooperation, you are setting yourself up for disillusionment. They don't want to be bothered by others' feelings or requests, so these people place a very high priority on protecting their privacy. You can't expect them to be sensitive to someone else's needs, because life is all about them. When you try to teach them otherwise, you will find yourself working with an unwilling student. If you keep trying persuasion, pleading, or coaxing, they will see that as an invitation to be stubborn, and you'll still be frustrated and upset. In fact, as passive-aggressive persons sense that you need their cooperation, it only fuels their feeling of power.

They actually enjoy knowing that they can frustrate you, and they will look for ways to prove that you cannot impose your desires on them. To them, discussions about feelings and needs mark the beginning of a competition to prove who is in the decision-making seat. (Hint: That person is not you.)

Barbara once told me, "I really don't mind being in a caregiving role with my dad. No, he wasn't perfect as a father, but who is? He still has plenty of qualities that make him a good man, and I feel privileged to show him in his latter years that I respect and honor him. I love him, and the least I can do is assist him in doing things he can no longer do for himself." Heaving a great sigh, she said, "I can't comprehend how Donald can justify being so stubborn when I ask him to pitch in and fulfill his family responsibility. I know he doesn't have as much spare time as I do, and I don't ask that he match my efforts with the same amount of time. I just wish I could get him to take *some* initiative. Is that expecting too much?"

There were two answers to Barbara's question. Appealing to common courtesy and fair play, no, she was not asking too much for her brother to be a loving family member. Factoring in Donald's history of chronic self-absorption, yes, she was asking too much. His character was not inclined toward courtesy and fairness. By allowing herself to dream that one day he would drop his unwillingness to engage fully with the family, she was ensuring that she would feel disillusioned.

Very few relationships operate with a perfectly balanced division of effort and initiative. It would be nice to know that in your closest relations, your conscientious attitudes would be matched by equally conscientious attitudes in the partner. Such a thought, however, is fantasy, not reality. Rarely do relationships operate with true fairness intact.

When you are involved with a narcissist, you will need to be quite vigilant regarding the role of leadership. Specifically, you cannot allow the narcissist to establish the rules of engagement. Your task will be to drop any requirements for fairness, establishing the pace of the relationship as best as it can be done. While you are not likely to coax wonderful responses from the narcissist, you can certainly maintain a positive influence despite the passive-aggressive person's disinterest.

As I spoke with Barbara about her response to Donald, I mentioned, "You cannot afford to have high expectations for his reform, because if you do, he will disappoint you virtually every time. The less you rely on his good attitude, the less disappointed you will be."

"But it seems so wrong that I should have no expectations, because he will just waltz off into the sunset doing his own thing, totally unconcerned about me or our dad."

"You're right about him waltzing off with unconcern," I responded, "but none of your efforts to date have proven that you are ever going to get him to see the light. Whether you plead or whether you let him be, he will be the same. Besides, at this point in your relationship with him, it would be best to drop any thoughts about fairness."

"If I hold zero expectations for him, I would feel like I am enabling very irresponsible behavior, and that really feels wrong," Barbara retorted.

"You're making the mistake that you can reason with him as you might with normal people," I responded. "I agree that it seems wrong to let him be whatever he wants to be, yet with or without your concurrence he will continue to mystify. Your feelings are quite normal, but I'm simply suggesting that we be as realistic as possible as we assess his behaviors. You are not enabling him by doing this; you are simply accepting that he is what he is."

Barbara eventually decided that she would greatly decrease the times when she would include Donald in her plans to assist their father. Recalling dozens of incidents when he failed to follow through on his promises, she had to admit that he was committed to being coy, and she was not going to be the one to make him give up his shady behavior. Instead, she would manage her efforts with their dad on her own terms. If he ever wanted to assist, he could let her know, and even then she could ultimately decide if she wanted to work with him.

"I feel like I'm giving up on him," she acknowledged, "when I drop all expectations. It just seems so unnecessary."

"In a sense we are indeed conceding that you might have to give up on him, at least as it relates to him being a caring contributor in family matters. He has such a deep history of noncompliance, though, that he leaves you little other option."

Because you naturally apply empathy and consideration, it can feel quite unnatural to accept that someone else can be so callused that they cannot do the same. Your struggle with such feelings implies that you are wishing to impose your values onto one who has no concern for them. As right as your values might be, you will only find disillusionment when you assume the narcissist will eventually match your good will.

### Guard Against Angry Reactions

Passive-aggressive narcissists find a perverse delight when they know they have generated strong responses of anger in others. As they witness how others fume or rage in response to their stubbornness, they indulge the thought, "This proves how you are inferior to me, and that means I control you." In a backward way, they think like the playground bully whose feeling of significance is enhanced each time he generates anxiety and doubt in those who dare to think or act upon separate notions. Narcissists need to know they are important, and your angry response validates that they remain in an influential position.

Somewhere along the way, passive-aggressive people came to believe that personal satisfaction couldn't be found by behaving according to normal standards. Feeling inadequate, they convinced themselves that goodness is not really good at all but a representation of someone else's effort to force conformity. Compensating for their own enormous self-doubt, they determined that others' values are worthless. That proof is gained each time their antagonist acts unruly, and upon witnessing the meltdown of others they then feel justified continuing in nonconformist ways.

Through the years, as Barbara tried to engage successfully with her brother, she had been prone to outbursts of anger. As teens she and Donald often had ugly disputes that included extended bickering and many insults. As adults, they learned to tame some of their adolescent misbehavior; yet even in her forties Barbara was still capable of popping off toward her brother when he was especially evasive. Just prior to talking with me about her dilemma, she had launched into strong words of rebuke toward Donald one Sunday afternoon after he had failed to get medicine at the pharmacy as he had promised. In front of her teenage son, she yelled at Donald using language not befitting a woman of her stature, while he merely stared blankly saying nothing.

Reflecting on that episode of anger, I asked Barbara, "How would you rate the success of the tirade? Did it produce any good results?"

Frowning and shaking her head in disgust, she replied, "Of course not. I never get any good results when I try to reason with that blockhead. He either has an airtight excuse for his behavior, or he turns the tables on me by commenting on my outrageous behaviors. I'm telling you, he is one slippery eel when it comes to any effort to pin him down."

"Barbara, your anger is not a wrong or irrational response to his behavior," I said. "Right now, though, I'm not so concerned about whether your emotions are justified as I am in helping you stay out of his emotional clutches. He is not a balanced person, and you have no reason to believe that his status will change anytime soon. That being the case, you can actually choose to lay down your anger and leave him alone."

Following up on the theme of dropping her expectations of good will from him, I added, "If there were any indication that he would be willing to hear your valid feelings, I would encourage you to speak truth to him in a way that he could understand. I think you would agree with me, though, that such an effort often represents wasted energy. In those incidents, let him go, and don't invest any more emotion in him."

"That seems so sad," she reflected. "I really believe in the need for families to stick with one another, but he can't seem to grasp the validity of that ideal."

"That's true, he can't grasp what you want him to grasp. In your anger, you want to correct an obvious wrong, but when he senses your anger, he turns the situation into a competition for power. In your continuing anger, you are indicating that you will compete for that power, but I am suggesting that you recognize such a competition as foolhardy."

In its best use, anger can lead to constructive dialogue that enhances the maturity of a relationship. (We'll elaborate on this notion in Chapter Six.) Passive-aggressive narcissists, however, are not mature. They cannot be expected to process feelings or conflicts with sound reason. While you cannot simply turn your anger off like a switch, you can learn to save your expressions of anger for times when they will be more personally rewarding.

As Barbara reflected on letting go of her anger toward Donald, she said, "I guess this means I am letting go of the hope for normalcy. It feels like I am letting go of my concerns for him, and I suppose that's what might be required. If he doesn't care about our family unity, why should I keep trying to be his conscience?" Barbara's reasoning, though indeed sad, was right on.

### Stop Yearning for Acceptance

Mature relationships operate on the basis of mutual satisfaction. Normal people recognize that the best way to gain understanding is to give away understanding. Likewise, the best way to be loved is to give love. A consistent commitment to a give-and-take process is a cornerstone for those wishing to find satisfaction in relationship.

Narcissists do not focus on the same goals as their more normal counterparts. They want power, and they certainly like to be in the position of uniqueness—and that is not the same as wanting mutual satisfaction. Remember, by definition, narcissists like to assume they are superior, and such thinking inhibits them from giving away acceptance, because that would require them to come down from their exalted perch.

When I asked Barbara to consider why she had allowed herself to tolerate her brother's passive abuse, she summarized, "Despite all his faults, he's still my brother. I have never wanted to give up on him, because that would mean admitting that there is little love to share."

"Let's put it this way," I said. "You will never have to let go of your commitment to be a loving sister, even if he never appreciates what you have to offer. Your ability to love does not have to be contingent on his responses. On the other hand, it would be wise to drop the fantasy that he will love you, at least not as you understand love to be. While it would be nice for him to join you as a full-fledged family member, he has proven that he is not interested. You do not *have to* have his acceptance or blessing to continue in your mission to be loving."

Like their hypercontrolling counterparts, passive-aggressive narcissists have airtight explanations for their behaviors and attitudes. You cannot expect to be loved by them until they lay down their contrived admiration for themselves, a prospect not likely to be achieved by your lecturing or persuading.

Given the fact that anger is such a common problem when relating with narcissists, we will dedicate a full chapter to further examination of the do's and don'ts of this emotion. You cannot afford to be overcome by chronic anger simply because the person in front of you chooses inappropriateness. Before we get to that chapter, we will discuss in Chapter Five how to avoid being caught in the snares of the narcissists' many demands.

## Chapter Five

# The Bottomless Well of Common
# Narcissistic Demands

Keith had gone to work with his dad, Judd, right out of college, helping him manage an air conditioning installation business. Before Keith hired on, the business was just barely breaking even. Keith had a great business sense that allowed him to develop and execute sweeping plans that helped the company to increase sales and earnings threefold in just a few years. About ten years later, Judd decided he wanted to retire, so they arranged for Keith to buy out his share of the company. After the transaction was complete, Judd struggled with allowing his son to function in the new role as CEO. Despite the poor state of the business when Keith came on board and the great results they had seen since his arrival, Judd could not seem to admit that he needed to step aside and let Keith be the sole decision maker. Not once in their ten years of working together had he been willing to compliment Keith for his many contributions or acknowledge his own flaws. Instead, Judd accused Keith of being disloyal and intimated that, as the founder and owner, he was really responsible for the company's success. He seemed solely concerned with making sure that Keith paid attention to his opinions and gave himself credit for all that Keith had accomplished. When Keith came to see me, he was demoralized and perplexed—and tired of trying to get along with his father and keep the business going.

Narcissists of any kind must be satisfied that they are in a position of status or privilege. They are unable to take a secondary role or to resist their impulses to draw attention to themselves. Passive-aggressive narcissists make attempts to remain uninvolved and detached, yet over time even they want to enforce their agendas. All narcissists want to impose their will on others through manipulation and demands. They are very hard to resist, so it's important to understand this component of their makeup if you want to learn to manage your responses to them in a way that will allow you to maintain your sanity and self-worth.

Responding to the narcissist's tendency to communicate in unbending terms is often a vicious cycle. Their demands often elicit protests and resistance, which irritates the narcissist, who then becomes even more stubborn and inflexible, making the other person increasingly frustrated and irritated. With each turn of the cycle and each additional exchange of agitated words, both people get even more annoyed. As the narcissist continues making demands, the recipient is likely to wonder, "What is *wrong* with this person?" Nothing seems to affect the narcissist. Does this cycle sound familiar?

Though they never voice it as an explicit goal, narcissists want to wear down the resolve of anyone who would dare to think or feel differently. They can become so overwhelming that their partners eventually appease them just to bring an end to the conflict and get some peace. That is exactly what narcissists want, and it encourages them to keep applying pressure tactics to get others to meet their demands. Though this cycle is vicious, it isn't inevitable. You can learn to assertively resist narcissistic demands and put an end to their efforts to impose their will on you. At first, as you begin to be assertive with a narcissist, you will likely experience short-term discomfort as they continue to pressure you. Don't be dissuaded. Maintain your resolve. You can choose to be firm in your responses, believing that your firmness will yield good results. Although the narcissist might or might not get the message and change, even if he or she doesn't, you will be able to maintain self-respect and freedom to act in ways that you know are wisest for you.

With that in mind, let's look at some of the more common narcissistic demands with the intent of determining the best ways to respond.

## "You Must Remain Loyal to Me"

Narcissists act as if people are their property. They have such a strong feeling of entitlement that they truly seem to believe that they own the people closest to them. For instance, a narcissistic spouse can be irrationally controlling, completely oblivious to the reality that it is reasonable for the mate to have separate priorities. Likewise, a narcissistic boss can treat employees like mechanical parts of a machine that can be exchanged on a whim, completely disregarding their feelings or needs. Narcissists are not willing to allow others to be autonomous, because they are convinced that their logic is so superior that it is all that is needed. When a partner of a narcissist attempts to branch out with independent choices, the narcissist is likely to protest, "You can't do this to me. You owe it to me to do as I want." While narcissists are hardly loyal toward those they exploit, they nonetheless demand loyalty in return.

In Keith and Judd's case, even when Keith's new ideas clearly generated increased revenues, Judd would complain that his son was being disloyal to him. For instance, Keith revamped the company's accounting system, pulling together separate departments of the company under one person's supervision. Instead of praising Keith for his good idea, Judd griped, "This is not the way I've done things in the past. Why do you have to undermine me?" In the strange logic of a narcissist, he saw Keith's improvements as disloyalty to the way Judd had run the company. He couldn't acknowledge how badly the company needed change; he could only focus on preserving his fragile ego.

In its best sense, *loyalty* can be understood as faithfulness to a cause or person. The narcissist, however, understands loyalty as the blind acquiescence of others to the narcissist's beliefs or preferences. There is no room for questions or changes. Others are simply supposed to follow the narcissist's lead, even at the cost of their better judgment. The narcissist interprets any inclination to chart a separate path as betrayal.

At times, people such as Keith can feel such pressure to remain loyal to the narcissist that they choose not to follow their good instincts. For instance, as Keith reorganized the company's policies and procedures, he had to ask key longtime employees to take on tasks that stretched their skills and required specialized training. Instead of complimenting him on generating cutting-edge practices, Judd repeatedly questioned, "Are you sure you need to do it that way?" His complaints were often so offensive and harsh that Keith questioned the validity of his decisions. His father could be very persuasive.

When you come under attack for disloyalty, it is wisest not to defend or to agree with the demands on the spot. Rather, you can allow yourself the time to reflect on the wisdom of your decisions, perhaps even talking to a trusted friend or an advisor so that you can maintain a broader perspective. Of course, the narcissist will hate that, but remember that your goal is not to keep the narcissist happy. Your goal is to follow common sense as you make your decisions.

Keith told me about many scenes from his childhood when his father dominated their family, ridiculing anyone who dared to differ with him. Judd often lectured them about the necessity of loyalty. Now as an adult who worked side by side with Judd, Keith recognized that his father was really looking for blind obedience. That was something he could not give him. He told Judd, "Now that I'm the owner of the company, I'm going to need the latitude to do things as I see fit, and I'm hoping that you'll be able to appreciate what I'm doing. If you can't, I still need to make decisions based on my own determinations."

Keith was loyal to good business practices, and he determined that if his dad could not understand that fact, he needed to proceed regardless of Judd's tirades. He came to understand that he could give himself permission to proceed with his good decisions with or without his father's blessing. He rightly recognized that it is not prudent to fight for a narcissist's approval because it will never come.

### "It's Never My Fault"

By definition, narcissists have little insight into their own person-alities. They have such a strong need to feel special that they do not recognize the extent (or sometimes even the presence) of their dys-functional behavior. They regularly minimize their negatives; when anyone dares to discuss their flaws openly, they predictably become angry and defensive. "Don't talk to me about my problems," is their cry. "If anyone around here is troubled, it is you, not me!" It is rare indeed for a narcissist to take full responsibly for the difficulties they create.

Keith had experienced this aspect of narcissistic behavior many times in his dealings with his father. "Ever since we've been in busi-ness together, I've discovered all sorts of little practices of his that are less than honorable," he explained. "He's not honest with cus-tomers or with subcontractors. He'll say whatever is convenient for the moment, then later he'll try to figure out how to dig out of the holes he gets into. I've confronted him several times about the need to shoot straight with the people we work with, and amazingly he implies that I'm the one with the problem because I don't under-stand the way business gets done."

From Keith's description, I could see that Judd practiced what I refer to as *boomerang communication*. Just as a boomerang reverses its path and heads back toward the thrower, so confrontations with a narcissist tend to land back on the one who confronts. Whereas secure individuals can hear feedback, even if it might feel uncom-fortable, narcissists refuse. Since they must always remain superior, they reason that they cannot be held responsible for any problem that arises. The fault must always be someone else's.

For people like Keith who are on the receiving end of the nar-cissist's accusations, it's natural to react defensively. Weary of taking the brunt of the narcissist's attacks and wishing to be heard, you might try to force the narcissist to agree or to gain a different insight. But that will only generate stronger counterattacks. Narcissists will never concede anything that sounds like defeat. Keith told me that one day he had been especially frustrated with Judd's slippery way of blaming him for problems that he did not generate. He felt tempted to lash out at his dad to explain how he needed to see his own part in the problem, but he wisely reconsidered. Remembering how past discussions had produced virtually no good results, Keith decided to disengage from the fruitless debate his father wanted to pull him into. "I told myself that there is no need to defend something that needs no defense. As a general rule, I like the way I do business, so if he wants to take shots at me, that is his prerogative. I don't need to engage in discussions that will end with him accusing me falsely."

Don't make the mistake of talking with narcissists about their flawed perceptions of you or a problem. Let them blame you, if that is what they must do, but don't heed them. If the narcissist continues to accuse you, you might have to accept that is the reality. You cannot correct them, but you can make good decisions—without that person's blessing.

## "Don't Tell Anyone About Our Problems"

With their fragile egos, narcissists don't want anyone to see or know about their flaws. Keeping an unblemished image is so vital to them that they will try to do so even if it requires that they hide their defects or become secretive. While it might be relatively easy to give a false positive impression to strangers, it's much harder to maintain a spotless image with close associates. Faced with exposure, narcissists will pressure their intimates to keep up the false front.

Sandi had struggled for years to contain the feelings of despair she felt due to her many conflicts with her husband, Justin. It was not at all uncommon for him to explode toward her just prior to a public event, only to have him insist that she smile and pretend that she felt fine once they were in others' presence. Because Sandi tended to be shy, Justin had taken her reluctant nature as an invitation to be imposing, but little did he know that his act was wearing thin and that she was ready to chart a new course. "I was constantly put in the position of having to be a phony," she told me, "because if I even hinted that I was feeling hurt or disappointed, he'd bring the full brunt of his wrath to bear on me once we got home." For instance, Justin knew Sandi admired her older sister, Kathy, and had a history of confiding personal matters to her. He sternly warned Sandi after their fights that she must not discuss their marital problems with Kathy. In years past, Sandi lived in fear that Justin would find out if she spoke honestly with Kathy, so she learned to keep things to herself.

When she talked with me about being pressured to prop up a false front in the presence of family and friends, I wanted to capitalize on her readiness to make significant changes in her responses to Justin. "Does it seem reasonable to speak about personal matters with someone like your sister, who loves you and has much support to offer?" Sandi nodded and mentioned that she was very confident in Kathy's discerning spirit. "We've each been there for one another when the chips were down," she said, "and I feel like I'm dishonoring our relationship when I have to keep so much of my life hidden from her," she told me.

I explained that it was reasonable for her to use tact as she discussed Justin's flaws with a trusted friend or relative, yet she was under no obligation to provide cover for him. That enabled his narcissism, and it helped keep alive the very traits in him that she disliked. "It really is okay for you to tell your sister when you are hurting," I explained. "I'm sure you would want to know of Kathy's pain if the roles were reversed. Living in an abusive marriage can generate feelings of loneliness and isolation, and you will become increasingly vulnerable to depression or bitterness if you have no one to give you emotional support."

Initially, Sandi was emotionally conflicted as we discussed her changing tactics. "But if Justin finds out that I've exposed our problems to someone, he'll be furious! I'll never hear the end of it."

"That anger is his way of illustrating that he wants no accountability for his actions," I mentioned. "Each time you go along with his demand to keep quiet about your problems, you are sending him the message that he can continue his overbearing treatment toward you. He can assume he will never have to answer to anyone. Is that really what you want to communicate?"

Sandi was not obligated to remain silent simply because her disclosures would create discomfort for Justin. She eventually concluded that it was not Justin's prerogative to determine how much or how little she would share with her sister. Once he learned that she intended to talk freely with Kathy, he predictably became angry and once again told her not to tell her sister anything about them or their relationship. Sandi, however, had braced herself for this reaction and had determined that she would not become drawn into a war of words with her husband. She simply replied, "When I feel the need to talk with Kathy about my life, I'll do so." No further explanation was needed. When he continued yelling his commands at her, she calmly but firmly held her ground, saying, "I plan to handle my relationship with Kathy in the way that makes the most sense to me."

When people such as Sandi make the mistake of keeping the narcissist's problems secret, they only prolong their own misery. You are not being unreasonable when you want to put your personal needs first rather than constantly capitulate to a narcissist's selfish mandates. Even when the narcissist becomes angry or threatening, you can remain true to your own common sense. There's no need to offer apology or defense; you can determine to live your life as an open book, with nothing to hide. In doing so, you break the narcissist's rules, but you also recognize that he or she does not set the rules in the first place.

## "I'm Not Supposed to Suffer"

Narcissists inflict plenty of pain upon those nearest them, though they are usually oblivious to the extent of the misery they generate—or they simply do not care. When they feel any discomfort, however, they protest loudly. It doesn't occur to them that those responses are inconsistent. The inability to empathize causes them to ignore others' suffering, while the desire for entitlement prompts them to insist upon favored treatment.

Narcissists define pain differently from the way the average person does. To them, pain means they are not getting their way, and the discomfort they feel is an extension of the need to remain in control. For instance, each person in an organization performs for the good of the whole; those tasks often involve self-sacrifice (of time or energy or even credit). Whether you are dealing with family or friends or work associates, there are going to be times when you will experience inconvenience as part of the package. Narcissists can interpret simple acts of sacrifice as painful, not because they are in fact painful, but because they thwart the narcissist's will. They interpret even reasonable deeds for the common good as an imposition. Their hurt or discomfort is an indication of their childish insistence that life is supposed to revolve solely around their desires. For narcissists who feel anger or pain at entirely reasonable demands or decisions, their response can be understood as an adult version of a toddler's temper tantrum.

Several months into his attempted retirement, Judd complained bitterly to Keith. "Letting go of the reins is more difficult than I thought it would be, and I'm miserable almost every day," he said. In one way, such a sentiment could be considered normal, since many seniors find it less than easy to let go of the life that had sustained them for decades. Yet in this case there was another dimension to consider. Judd had a deep history of being controlling to the point of micromanaging those nearest him. He commonly griped when he did not get his way, and he accused others of making his life difficult when they were simply acting autonomously. Indeed, he often seemed unhappy, but not because of others' insensitivities. He was unable to recognize that his demanding spirit was the primary source of his pain. His complaint, then, about struggling to let go of the business illustrated that he had never learned that he could find contentment when he was not in control.

While Keith worked hard to be fair-minded and objective, he nonetheless struggled at times to come to terms with Judd's misery. "I've known for a long time that it is not my job to keep Dad happy.

He's been irritable and grouchy for as long as I've known him, and as I've aged I have been able to understand that he has demons in his closet that he's never come to terms with. But I swear, he's a master at manipulating people's emotions, including mine, to get them to think that they are the ones responsible for his chronically painful moods." Each time Judd accused him of causing him pain because he was operating with a different business philosophy, Keith had to remind himself that Judd wasn't talking about the business but about his own ego. Keith could choose to continue with his plans even if it meant ignoring his father's opinions or wishes, and he wasn't being a cold-hearted person for doing so. He was merely living with his own sound convictions.

People such as Keith often want to please others by showing consideration for their emotional burdens. Not only is this not a bad way to live, it can be an indication of a commitment to love and goodness. Narcissists, however, take advantage of this empathy and compassion. People in Keith's position, then, will need to balance their naturally sympathetic outlook with firm resolve. The narcissist's complaints do not have to get highest priority in making decisions. Common sense and appropriate self-preservation can take precedence.

## "I'm the Center of Everything"

By nature, human beings are interdependent. As we constructively consider how to work and live with the decisions, feelings, and needs of those nearest to us, we promote good will, and we find peace in the process. Healthy individuals maintain a habit of monitoring the lives of those nearest them, not for the purpose of being snoopy or controlling but to know how to coordinate with them. As an illustration, suppose a husband determines to spend a Saturday running errands and doing menial chores around the house. Before getting his day started, he checks with his family to learn their plans and makes necessary amendments to his own, if necessary. In doing so, he demonstrates an awareness that his life is interconnected with his family's and that he gladly considers their needs and plans as he also acts upon his own.

Narcissists do not operate this way. Sometimes they will choose to coordinate their lives with others, yet even when their behaviors seem friendly they might be positioning themselves to get their own way. Most of the time, they make unilateral decisions without much concern for how those decisions affect others. Instead of thinking "I need to coordinate my life with them," they think, "They'll just have to adjust to me."

One Thursday evening, Judd phoned to ask if Keith and his son would be interested in spending the weekend hunting with him. Keith enjoyed the outdoors and thanked Judd for the offer, but explained he already had plans related to his son's Boy Scout group. Later, as Judd was moping around his house, Judd's wife asked him why he was so moody. Judd snarled, "First he wrangles my company away from me, then he stiff-arms me when I try to include him in an enjoyable outing. That boy is ruining my life." Never mind that Keith was trying to be a supportive father to his own son. His dad was only focused on making Keith do his bidding. That's the way a narcissist's mind works.

When Keith later learned that his father was frustrated about being spurned, he immediately wanted to pick up the telephone and talk him out of his foul mood. Reason quickly caught up with him, though, as he reminded himself, "This is typical of his reactions when he does not get his way. Dad has rarely been willing to factor in my needs as we try to decide how to coordinate our plans. Why should I expect that he will hear what I have to say about the subject this time?" Keith rightly determined that he did not need to justify his decision to participate in his son's Boy Scout venture. Several days later, when he asked Judd about the hunting weekend, his dad offered a curt reply. Again Keith was tempted to plead his case, but again he determined that if Judd needed to feel bitter, it was not his problem to solve.

Narcissists anchor on the question, "What are you going to do to make my day go better?" For a narcissist, team spirit is a foreign concept; little else matters beyond his or her circumstances. Narcissists are likely to use guilt to wrangle you into compliance, but you can choose to remain firm as you pursue your own plans. You don't need to fall for the narcissistic assumption that he or she is the only one with valid needs.

## "The Rules Don't Apply to Me"

Sandi had begun counseling after she learned that her husband, Justin, had two affairs that she knew of and that he frequented strip clubs and porn sites on the Internet. He initially expressed regret and promised that he would do whatever it took to restore her trust in him. In one of our initial sessions, I had emphasized that Justin would need to remove what I refer to as "the two D's": deception and deservedness. He would need to treat all aspects of his life as an open book, and he would need to lay down any requests for favored treatment and entitlements. We had also discussed the wisdom of becoming involved in a Twelve-Step group that would prompt him to confront the addictive elements in his behaviors. He would need to be serious about taking the lead in demonstrating his willingness to curtail his cravings so he could become the family man he said he wanted to be.

Justin seemed somewhat reluctant to go along with the strict accountability that was implied in the parameters we established, but he declared that he did not want a divorce and that he would do whatever it took to get back into Sandi's good graces. In just a few weeks, however, Justin began backpedaling on his agreement. One Saturday, Sandi was sorting through the family bills and looked carefully at his cell phone records. One number seemed suspicious, and when she asked about it, he seemed annoyed that he would be required to explain it. When she requested that he show her his work-related expense statements, he balked again, stating that he did not believe it was really necessary to produce them. And after going to one Twelve-Step meeting, he declared that such a program was not for him. "I don't know why you think it's necessary to scrutinize every aspect of my life," he sneered at Sandi. "I'm not used to having someone breathe down my neck all the time."

In a follow-up counseling session, I told them that it indeed was reasonable for Sandi to ask that Justin be accountable, given the nature of his misbehaviors. "Besides," I explained, "when a man and woman marry, it is reasonable to assume that you are one unit. In its best sense, mutual accountability helps you feel like you're a part of each other's worlds and that you each make decisions in consideration of the other. It will be good for you to learn to appreciate this fully."

Justin spoke abruptly, "I don't like being given a bunch of rules. I'm my own person, and I want to feel like I can make decisions without the threat of being vetoed." His face had become quite flushed.

Far from insisting that Justin and Sandi should have a harsh, rules-oriented way of life, I had simply appealed to common sense as we tried to determine how to set their relationship back on course. I had expressed the belief that it is good to have well-defined standards as part of their relationship. Justin nonetheless interpreted my suggestions concerning openness and accountability as confining to him. He wanted little to do with it. "Maybe other guys feel okay about giving their wives that kind of power," he said, "but that's not for me." He was very unaccustomed to having anyone else establish standards for his life.

Justin was exhibiting a sociopathic attitude, which is not uncommon in narcissists. People with this tendency assume that morality is relative, that they can pick and choose whatever rules they want to live by without having to heed outside authority. If the rules hinder their desires, they reserve the right to rewrite the rulebook or to ignore it completely. While they might superficially agree that firm standards are good, they inevitably display a disdain for authority and openness. They like to keep all options open, and they reject the notion that anyone else should keep them accountable. When narcissists refuse to accept reasonable standards, it's useless to plead your case or debate the merits of your cause. They're unlikely to pay any attention to your ideas, and it is unlikely that you will win any verbal battles. Instead, holding them accountable to the consequences of their actions is one of the few ways to convey the message that you intend to be taken seriously. Boundaries and stipulations can be established, not as a means of controlling, but to show that you intend to be seriously considered. For instance, Sandi spoke quite firmly with Justin as it became clearer that he did not intend to be held accountable. "Even though you say that you want to keep the marriage together, I'm going to need to see evidence that you truly mean it." She then added, "If you decide that you want to continue living without legitimate restraints, we will have to reconsider whether the marriage can continue. I've been through enough grief as it is, and I'm not going to be able to tolerate your secrecy any longer."

Because narcissists like being in tight control, they are likely to protest greatly when someone applies consequences. They will likely express outrage, but usually that rage is a cover for panic. Your task will be to refrain from responding to their strong emotion with your own strong emotion. For instance, if you set a consequence with a narcissist, and you receive the predictable complaints, you can firmly but calmly state, "I know you don't like what I am requesting, but I intend to stand firm on my decision." When they continue to protest, you can again state, "I'm fully aware that you and I differ in the way we think about this, but I'm resolved." It's not necessary for you to plead or persuade. Let the validity of your reasonableness stand on its own, then be prepared to follow through on your consequences if necessary.

## "I Know Best—Do It My Way"

While narcissists strongly resist directives from others, they love having others bow to them. They are so enamored of their own special status that they are convinced that others' lives would be much better if they would give them control. This explains why they can be persuasive, stubborn, and bossy. They are blind to the inappropriateness of their "know-it-all" attitude.

Before Keith stepped into the management of his dad's air conditioning company, Judd struggled to keep the business going. There was plenty of work, but he was not good with marketing, and he had difficulty retaining reliable employees. Keith, however, had a strong knack for finding new business and knowing how to present proposals relating to customers in a manner that inspired their confidence. He succeeded in hiring reliable employees who represented the company well. Those qualities and his talents saved what was probably a failing business. Despite the stark contrast between Judd's business practices and Keith's, Judd seemed convinced that his son should consult him in virtually all decisions. In the early days of learning the in's and out's of the air conditioning business, Keith indeed made efforts to draw upon his father's years of experience. Though he had not demonstrated a keen entrepreneurial sense, Judd knew plenty of people and could be valuable in explaining nuances to Keith. Once Keith began developing contacts and knowledge on his own right, Judd remained unconvinced that his son could do well without his ongoing advice, even though profits were way up, and the future was as secure as it had ever been. Still Judd could not give Keith the credit he was due.

Even after the buyout, Judd insisted that Keith should give him regular reports regarding near-term plans. He wanted to make sure his son was doing things right. Initially Keith complied with Judd's wishes out of courtesy, but over time, he felt less and less inclined to check his plans with his father, because he simply didn't want the barrage of unsolicited advice that was sure to come. As his father sensed Keith pulling back, he became more demanding, even shouting and cursing when Keith made it clear that he was doing well enough on his own.

After many confrontations with his dad, Keith decided that it was time to explain his plan clearly, with the understanding that this would be his final conversation on the subject with him. He told Judd, "I know you feel strongly connected to the business, and I can certainly understand why. At the same time, I need you to understand that I'm the one who has the final say in day-to-day matters. You've been very free to offer advice that I have not needed, and I'm letting you know that I'm no longer going to be as congenial as I have been in the past. We've got a good thing going here at the office, and I intend to stay the course that has been established. I'll not be taking your calls as I have in the past because I don't want to be subjected to your criticisms and your outbursts. I also will not be keeping you as informed about daily business matters, not because I am trying to be secretive, but because it has proven to be too stressful to continue communicating with you about the business." Keith was both calm and firm as he spoke.

Judd could tell there was a definite difference in the way his son was talking to him. When he protested that Keith was talking like an insubordinate person, Keith firmly reminded him that he was no longer in the subordinate position. Those days were gone. As time progressed, Judd repeatedly complained about Keith's lack of appreciation, and he insinuated that he should consult him more often, but Keith held firm.

Following another's advice and direction can be a positive characteristic in many relationships, in the sense that it indicates both humility and team spirit. It doesn't mean you have to stop having opinions or assertions, but it encourages respect—not blind loyalty or lack of initiative. For instance, Keith's father would have preferred him to acquiesce to his directives even at the expense of the company's growth. That was obviously not wise. When someone such as Judd demands others' complete obedience, they often confuse subordination with subservience. Narcissists, with their strong sense of entitlement, are likely to forget that subordination works best when the entire organization (be it a business, family, church, government) is committed to the common good.

## Who Calls the Shots?

The longer you interact with a narcissist, the more likely it is that you will engage in power struggles for control. People such as Keith and Sandi routinely report fatigue at having constantly to battle with narcissists who feel they must impose their will on every element of life. I remind them that they have a free will (something narcissists like to ignore), and despite the narcissist's protest, they can and should exercise their prerogative to choose other paths and options. When the narcissist becomes adversarial, you are under no obligation to get their agreement. Contrary to the narcissist's desire, you get to determine how to proceed with your plans. Failure to be true to yourself will become the first step toward your own irrational anger, depression, and anxiety, as we will see in Part Three, which is devoted to helping you gain greater skill in managing the narcissists in your life.

Part Three

# Dealing with the Narcissists in Your Life

## Chapter Six

# Examining Your Anger

Whether the narcissist in your life is hypercontrolling or passive-aggressive, you have probably experienced more than your fair share of anger. While you might be reluctant to reveal publicly the extent of your anger, you might well harbor deep feelings of bitterness, hatred, or resentment, and you cannot afford to let them rule your life. Part of your effort to respond appropriately to the narcissists in your life includes developing the skills to manage your anger appropriately.

As we have discussed in earlier chapters, anger is an understandable reaction to narcissists. But most people are not skilled in managing their anger when it arises in response to a narcissist's manipulations, nor have they examined how anger fits in to their broader vision of life. Most people have not taken the time to contemplate the purposes and uses of their anger, and the result is an emotional system that runs amok.

Josh sat in front of me shaking his head as he described why he had sought counseling. "Three years ago I divorced Carrie, hoping I would be able to get away from her erratic behaviors, but in a sense my problems are worse now than before." He went on to explain that in their nineteen years of marriage, she had displayed a combination of hypercontrolling behavior and passivity. Sometimes Carrie would be abnormally critical and explosive, while at other times she would become sullen and distant. "I never knew what I would be coming home to," Josh told me. "There were actually times when I thought we were doing okay, but then she would lay into me with some sort of complaint that seemed miniscule, and we'd be off to the races with major arguments. Other times I would notice that she was upset, so I'd try to be a good husband and talk out feelings with her, but she would take it as an opportunity to brush me off and wouldn't speak to me. She was incredibly moody, and I was not successful in learning how to blend my needs with hers. We were like oil and water."

In my ongoing discussions with Josh, it became apparent that Carrie had strong narcissistic tendencies. While Josh was not always the picture of perfection, he made solid attempts to be considerate, and he read books and went to seminars to learn how to be more effective in their marriage. Occasionally Carrie would indicate interest in exploring the personal dimensions of their marriage, but more commonly she belittled people in the helping professions by saying insulting things about them. She had little need for input from outsiders, though she was quick to agree that Josh could use all the help he could find. She was a very demanding person and took little guidance from anyone. *Smug* would be an apt description for the manner she adopted in public.

Josh told me that Carrie seemed to have an almost total inability to love. "I am definitely capable of saying the wrong thing or being insensitive at times, but I'm no imbecile either," he explained. "I put a high premium on displaying good character, but in my ex-wife's view, I was never good enough. For the last several years of our marriage she could not say the words 'I love you,' and she refused to be sexual with me. She projected a friendly image in public, yet behind the scenes she would ridicule anyone and everyone. She was so enormously impressed with herself that no one outside a small circle of people could meet her criteria for acceptance. Once she sees a person's imperfections, she marks them off her list and has nothing more to do with them.

"Since we've been apart, Carrie has seemingly made it her goal in life to destroy me," Josh continued. "She will drag out mistakes I made fifteen years ago and talk about them in great detail as if they happened just yesterday. I hear all sorts of stories through the grapevine about how she slanders me, and if that were the only problem, I could deal with it." Then shaking his head, he said, "Now it is clear that she has been feeding her poison to our sixteen-year-old daughter, openly trying to turn her against me. We have an eighteen-year-old son who just left home for college, and he and I have a solid relationship, but my daughter, Tracie, has become very confused and rebellious. Her mother has been so controlling toward her that she wants to lash out at the world. She's harder and harder to be around."

Josh was candid in telling me about his past wrongs, and I came to believe that he was being reasonably objective as he described his relationship with Carrie. Indeed, he was in an unenviable situation because she seemed so unwilling to forgive and to work to ensure that both their children enjoyed good relations with each parent. It seemed that she had fostered a spirit of competitiveness for their children's loyalties. She seemed unable to bear the thought that her daughter could have loyalties to anyone other than her.

True to the nature of narcissists, Carrie felt she was entitled to privileged treatment; in this case, that meant she would not compromise when Josh appealed to her to reconsider her parenting habits. Even members of Carrie's own family advised her to be more flexible with their daughter, but Carrie insisted that she knew what was best. Josh tried repeatedly to speak with her about being fair, but their conversations commonly ended with her being so histrionic and irrational that it only made the problems worse. "I honestly don't know what to do," Josh told me. "My daughter is more argumentative than ever before, and she refuses to discuss family matters with me because she is afraid to say anything that might get back to her mother. The poor kid is held captive by her mom's demanding spirit, and in the meantime I'm feeling emotionally tormented."

I realized that if Josh and I focused exclusively on Carrie's problems, we would succeed only in empty intellectualizing. To make the most of our counseling sessions, we needed to focus on the one person Josh could influence: himself. I said, "Josh, I don't envy you having to go through these trials and tribulations. I'm hearing that you are feeling a lot of pain and are baffled by your ex-wife's priorities. Though we will never succeed in making Carrie conform to your liking, we can still make headway by addressing how you will sift through your raw emotions."

"I'll openly admit that I struggle with lots of anger," he replied. "The funny thing is that I have never been prone to much anger outside my relationship with Carrie, but she can push my buttons like no one before or since."

Like Josh, you might have simmering struggles with anger as you try to make sense of another person's narcissism. Because narcissists are so unable to take any feedback or offer understanding and respect, you are likely to have deep feelings of futility. Whereas healthy relationships are typified by the willingness to address each person's concerns, that is not going to happen with narcissists. They are persistently unwilling to consider thoughts that conflict with their own.

## The Many Faces of Anger

It's common to assume that anger always takes the same form: shouting, slamming doors, ranting, accusing, and the like. If someone isn't behaving in those ways, so the stereotype goes, they are not really angry. Anger, however, takes many other forms. Anger may indeed be expressed in loud, raucous, aggressive behavior, but frustration, annoyance, fretting, muttering, criticism, and a host of other behaviors can also be manifestations of angry feelings. It is so broad and hard to categorize that the first step in taming it is to develop a full understanding of its presence in your life.

To gain perspective on the breadth of anger, look over the following list of behaviors closely associated with anger that has gone sour. Which ones have you experienced?

| | |
|---|---|
| Accusations | Chronic frustration |
| Annoyance | Coerciveness |
| Bickering | Complaining |
| Bitterness | Criticism |
| Bluntness | Disillusionment |

| | |
|---|---|
| Disobedience | Noncompliance |
| Dominance | Procrastination |
| Evasiveness | Pushy communication |
| Excessive defensiveness | Quitting |
| Fretting | Repetitive speech |
| Grouchiness | Resentment |
| Half-hearted efforts | Sarcasm |
| Impatience | Secretive misbehavior |
| Indifference | Sharp, abrupt speech |
| Invalidating others | Shutting down |
| Lack of mercy | Stubbornness |
| Meanness | Whining |
| Name calling | Withdrawal |

Chances are, you can admit to expressing your anger in many of the ways listed above, and you might even be able to add a few more. While it might surprise you that anger can take so many forms—and you might not find them all that flattering—you'll be much more able to bring it under control if you fully admit its presence in your life and avoid unproductive ways of managing it. Regardless of the forms it takes, even when it is unruly, anger is basically a drive for self-preservation. You do not experience anger in the presence of friendliness, cooperation, affirmation, or encouragement. Rather, you feel anger when you are faced with undesirable circumstances and situations that involve criticism, contrariness, griping, argumentativeness, and rejection. Behind anger is a cry for personal validation. Angry individuals contend that their needs are not being properly recognized and that others do not respect their core beliefs and values. In their anger, they wish to stand up for personal worth, dignity, and recognition.

Managed properly, anger can be a beneficial emotion in that it prompts us to stand firmly for the things we believe. It can compel us to address issues in ways that can promote harmony. Anger can be the beginning of efforts to correct problems and instill account-ability into relationships.

But despite its potential for good, anger tends to be more de-structive than constructive when individuals do not make the nec-essary efforts to channel it effectively. In the effort to preserve their personal needs or convictions, too many people might be so blunt and forceful (or even insulting) that their good message is poorly re-ceived. Sometimes anger can be accompanied by devious efforts to sabotage others' plans; sometimes it hides behind a judgmental spirit and eventually turns into bitterness and malice. The poten-tial misuse of anger is so great that we must ensure that its expres-sion does not lead to long-standing patterns of dysfunction.

For narcissists, anger is virtually never managed constructively. Whereas healthy anger can be instrumental in clearing relationships of strain and tension, narcissistic anger is not concerned with any-one else's needs. Narcissists only want to be vindicated and treated specially, so they cannot be trusted to be mature when explaining how they feel or what they want. If a narcissist provokes you to anger, be careful and determined not to match that person's inap-propriate anger with your own. The narcissist is not in charge of your emotions; you are.

As I spoke with Josh about the lingering emotional effects of his relationship with Carrie, he told me, "When we lived together, I frequently felt that Carrie was in a manipulation mode with me, es-pecially when we had separate ideas. She could become angry at the drop of a hat, and I never quite knew where her anger would lead. Sometimes she would launch into an all-out attack against my character, while at other times she would pretend to be calm, know-ing she could undermine me by not cooperating."

Shaking his head, Josh admitted, "I sometimes made our con-flicts worse by becoming sarcastic or argumentative with her. I would try to go into our discussions calmly, but as it became clear that she was only interested in her perspectives, my voice would rise and before you knew it, I could be yelling like a jerk. I'd tell myself that I couldn't afford to let her push my buttons, but I'd slip and get drawn into ways of communicating that would come back to haunt me."

Like Josh, perhaps you can recall moments when you allowed a narcissist to provoke the worst in your anger. While it's not unreasonable to get angry, the liability is that your valid message gets lost in the destructive behavior that accompanies it. To keep your anger from becoming destructive, it is helpful to consider that you have choices, both good and bad, in how you behave once your anger is aroused. By thinking in terms of choice, you can be more inclined to use reason to keep anger in check. You can also begin the process of reclaiming your emotional composure.

## Five Responses to Anger

In counseling Josh, I talked with him about five distinct options for handling his anger. It was up to him to sift through each one as he determined the best ways to respond to his ex-wife's frustrating ways. He told me, "I've never really thought about the possibility of having options when I feel ticked off or frustrated. My emotions just flow, and my habits overcome me so easily that I don't even think about what I'm doing or saying."

"Sure enough, you can be so used to your habitual ways of managing anger that you are hardly aware that you are making choices each time you feel angry," I replied. "Yet if we look at it more closely, you'll see that you do indeed choose how you will conduct yourself in the midst of your emotions. In fact, if your emotions were truly a matter of impulsive reactions, that would spell doom. You would have no capacity to grow and improve. You'd be stuck with behaviors that you have no control over. Only as we recognize that we have choices can we learn to maneuver through the difficulties of anger."

Since narcissists lack insight into their emotions, it is unlikely that they will think deeply about why they respond to conflict as they do. If they pause long enough to think about their angry expressions, it is usually with a spirit of blame. "Who is to blame for putting me in this foul mood?" they wonder. Then they expend their energies on efforts to manipulate others to do their bidding.

Rather than getting ensnared in a futile tit for tat, your efforts will be better spent looking inward to determine how to keep anger from turning into a colossal problem. Let's examine the forms that anger can take and your options for handling your responses.

## 1. Giving Up: Suppressed Anger

In any conflict it's always possible that feelings will be hurt and misunderstandings might occur. This is especially true when your antagonist is narcissistic. Instead of weighing carefully what you say and feel, narcissists will instinctively look for holes in your logic and attack you. They'll want you to give up your perspectives and take on theirs; if you show that you're holding firm, they'll see that as combativeness. You might legitimately get angry in such a conflict, but they don't care. In the narcissist's world, nothing matters beyond their feelings or declarations.

Knowing that the narcissist will likely ignore your feelings, it can be tempting to suppress them. You might rationalize that expressing your feelings would create more problems than it would solve, so you opt to hold them in. At the very least, if you suppress your feelings, you buy time to consider your next move. Yet rarely does this option resolve your anger. It is only a delaying tactic that generates further problems.

"Since we divorced," Josh recalled, "I have had one opportunity after another to address problems with Carrie. Most of our conflicts arise over problems we're having with Tracie or with money matters. I swear, I can hardly begin speaking, and she is already arguing with me. She's a mean woman, and she has to have full control of any decision that we make. I become so frustrated when dealing with her that I just give in way too easily. You can't get through to her!" He could recall numerous times when he simply gave up talking with her, letting her feel victorious. All the while, his hidden anger fed chronically bitter feelings. In his own words he felt "like a wimp" each time he conceded to her, and he assumed that he had no other choice than to let her have her way. He knew she would never let go of her headstrong ways.

Josh was definitely in a disadvantaged position, yet I was concerned that his inclination to suppress his anger was taking a toll on his quality of life. I was under no illusion that he could learn to say the right words to shape Carrie's behavior in a more positive direction, but I sensed that he was short-circuiting his legitimate needs. I wanted him to understand that by suppressing his anger, he was trading one set of problems in for another.

When you suppress your anger, it does not simply go away. Like water finding its way into a wall from a roof leak, it drips into other parts of your personality and damages you. For instance, suppressed anger is commonly behind the struggle with depression, which is fueled by feelings of defeat due to patterns of loss and invalidation. Suppressed anger also feeds anxiety, disillusionment, bitterness, and cynicism. When you suppress your anger, you are saying to yourself that self-preservation is too much trouble, and ultimately you are giving yourself a vote of no confidence. If you choose repeatedly to deny the legitimacy of your emotions and convictions, you will likely find that you're being equally ineffective in your other relationships as well.

## 2. Ranting and Raving: Openly Aggressive Anger

When most people think of anger, they are usually thinking of open aggression. Whereas anger represents the desire to stand up for legitimate worth, needs, and convictions, aggressive anger is behind inconsiderate and harmful behavior such as yelling, cursing, accusing, arguing, acting rebellious, pleading, asking loaded questions, inducing guilt, and shaming. Aggressive anger might have a legitimate cause at its base, yet its expression sabotages the good that might otherwise come from it.

People who are being openly aggressive in expressing anger make the mistake of assuming they can force the other person to change his or her mind or feelings. Of course, they rarely succeed, yet that does not stop them from attempting to gain power over their adversaries. When someone is being openly aggressive, logic and reason tend to go flying out of the window. What matters most to aggressive people is coercion.

Though Josh was not naturally inclined to be aggressive in expressing his anger, if his frustration built up, he could launch into strongly worded lectures. Carrie had a knack for baiting him with insults or stubborn refusals to listen. She frequently interrupted him when they discussed their differences, which caused Josh to feel belittled. Then he would blast her verbally for her selfishness, ridicule her lack of logic, or comment sarcastically on the worthlessness of her ideas. A few times he resorted to name calling. His voice could become firm to the point of being abrasive, and he would let her know in no uncertain terms that she was foolish for thinking as she did.

As we discussed his emotional responses to Carrie, I asked him to identify the elements in his anger that made sense. He seemed somewhat surprised by my question because he had assumed that poorly expressed anger was wrong in all aspects. Deeper reflection, however, caused him to recognize that indeed his ideas were legitimate. For instance, he believed that he should speak constructive (not shaming) words to his ex-wife when she was acting defiantly. Also, when they disagreed, he was being entirely reasonable in wanting to seek a fair middle ground and asking her to follow his lead to compromise. "There are plenty of right beliefs that lay beneath your feelings of anger," I commented, "but apparently you can be so forceful in the ways you try to gain her understanding that she will have nothing to do with them. Your overpowering and aggressive style of expressing anger allows her to justify her stubbornness."

"I try and try to maintain my cool when we have to discuss differences, but she is so self-righteous and so condescending toward me that it feels impossible to remain rational. Sometimes I just want to slap her! I know I shouldn't say that, but that is really how I feel."

Josh's admission is typical of those whose contentions with narcissists leave them feeling powerless to generate an atmosphere of reason or fairness. That feeling is legitimate, but they are taking cues from the narcissist's selfishness. They express their own selfish urges in hostile and aggressive ways. People such as Josh will be able to curb their aggressive expressions only if they remind themselves that they can choose to respond that way, but it's not the best option. The key point to remember is that they are under no obligation to set aside common sense and mirror the narcissist's gross insensitivity.

### 3. Going Underground: Passive-Aggressive Anger

Like other forms of anger, passive-aggressive anger (refusing to speak, quietly not complying, avoiding contact, and gossiping behind others' backs) is founded upon the desire to stand up for personal needs and convictions, though it is accompanied by noncompliant and frustrating behaviors. And like aggression, this kind of anger can be damaging to those on the receiving end. But the added element of passivity cloaks this expression of anger in deviousness and shields the angry person from having to be accountable for his or her actions. In a typical scenario, someone who expresses anger passive-aggressively is actually taunting, as if making the other person explode first allows them to heap blame and shame on him or her for the outburst.

Josh had a reputation for being an easygoing, levelheaded person. While he had had moments of open aggression, his prevailing tendency to suppress anger often led him to store up the emotion until it eventually caused him to become sullen and withdrawn. He explained, "Both during and after my marriage to Carrie, I never felt it would do any good to talk about my preferences because of her pure self-centeredness. There would be times when I'd deliberately stay away from the house for hours at a time just so I didn't have to be around her. Lots of times she would give me a long list of things to do, and I'd tell her what she wanted to hear (that I'd do them), knowing I would do whatever I felt once she was out of sight. Now that we live separate lives, I might go days before returning her phone calls, and I'll resist the chance to speak with her about pending matters, if for no other reason than to let her stew for a while."

"I suppose you realize that you are describing classic passive-aggressive behavior," I told Josh. He nodded and explained that sometimes he knew no other way to handle his emotions. I said, "I'm going to assume that as long as you know Carrie, you will be able to find reasons for handling your anger this way. By using passive means to punish her, you are playing right into her hands. She will rationalize that she can be as ugly as she wants because you have been inappropriate. Your passivity just keeps the game alive."

"I know it does," he admitted, "but what other options do I have? It is such a guarantee that she will be unreasonable that I feel like I'm stuck in a hole."

I was glad he asked that question, because it proved to be a perfect segue to discuss assertiveness as another option for managing his anger.

### 4. Firm and Fair: Assertive Anger

Often people believe assertiveness to be the same as aggressiveness. They mistakenly assume that assertiveness means they should be permitted to say whatever they want in any way they feel, and if the other person doesn't like it, too bad. Such an approach to anger management is not assertiveness at all—it is indeed an act of aggressiveness.

Assertiveness, like other expressions of anger, is yet another way to stand firm for personal needs and beliefs, but it has the added dimension of being respectful toward other people. When assertiveness is used properly, all those involved can maintain their dignity, and the anger is managed to create a more favorable outcome for everyone. Its purposes are constructive, not destructive. Assertive people realize that conflict in most close relationships does not need to be accompanied by a mean or vindictive spirit.

Sometimes people will ask: "Do I have a right to be angry?" With assertiveness, however, the question becomes, "Do I have the responsibility to be angry?" When you focus only on your rights, you are emphasizing only self-gratification, but when you focus on re-

sponsibilities, you can emphasize both your and others' needs. Assertive people know that they can most consistently stand up for
themselves in a constructive way when they leave open the possibility that the others can benefit from the exchange too.

As a response to anger, assertiveness can take various forms:

- Speaking firmly and to the point
- Holding your ground in the face of opposition
- Giving priority to your own common sense instead of acqui-
  escing to someone else's demands
- Saying "no" when necessary, even if it is unpopular
- Establishing personal preferences and stipulations
- Doing what you know is right even when others tell you to do
  differently
- Applying consequences when others are contrary
- Talking about difficult issues even if it might generate discomfort
- Acting immediately to address problems rather than letting
  them simmer
- Remaining consistent in your convictions; letting your yes
  mean yes or your no mean no

By managing your anger with assertiveness, you are letting others know that you believe in yourself and that you want to be
deemed credible. You need not use a harsh tone of voice, nor do you
have to be overly persuasive. With calm confidence, you can indicate that you believe in the legitimacy of your needs and convictions while still behaving in a respectful manner toward others.
People such as Josh who interact regularly with narcissists find assertiveness difficult, or at least less than satisfactory because it requires self-restraint. In the face of a narcissist's strongly aggressive
behavior or passive-aggressive manipulation, it's a great temptation
to respond in kind and unload anger aggressively. This predictably
creates a vicious cycle of more anger and unhealthy communication.
Narcissists are so unable to see any of your messages as legitimate

that you might conclude that assertive expressions of anger don't work any better than any other responses.

Josh told me, "While we were married, I felt like I was open to any reasonable suggestion that would help me respond appropriately to Carrie's moodiness. I'd try to be calm but firm. I used consequences. I'd state my needs in blame-free ways. I'd be sensitive about when I confronted her. But nothing worked with that woman! All she ever did in response to my efforts was to argue or tune me out."

Listening to Josh, I zoomed in on his use of the phrase *nothing worked*. That implied to me that he expected a specific positive outcome when he used assertiveness appropriately. I mentioned this to him, and he responded, "Well, yeah, I wanted her to realize that my purposes were honorable and that she should respond like a mature adult."

"How often did she reply to your assertiveness maturely?"

"Let's just say that I'm still waiting for that to happen. You don't have conflict with someone like her without it turning into a totally unnecessary battle."

Once you attempt to handle anger assertively but receive a poor response from the other person, you might conclude, as Josh did, that assertiveness is useless. However, before you collapse in defeat, think about why you are being assertive. The assertive communication of anger comes with no guarantee that the other person will receive it well. You might behave responsibly, but the narcissist might not. In fact, it is likely narcissists will try to turn your appropriate assertiveness against you. They can become highly defensive. They can blame or use denial. They can cry or run away. They can say whatever is expedient in the moment to appease you. They can be openly disrespectful toward your needs and convictions. In fact, even after several episodes of being assertive, none of your attempts might generate an appropriate response.

If assertiveness is such a great way of managing anger, why doesn't it elicit better responses from narcissists? The answer should be starting to be clear by now: narcissists are so self-absorbed that they consider few thoughts beyond those that suit their own purposes. They are predisposed to discount any confrontation, no matter how reasonable it might be. Narcissists simply do not care what you think, no matter how well you communicate.

If that's the case, why choose to be assertive with narcissists? The answer is that assertiveness is still the best way to manage and express anger, regardless of how the narcissist responds. Your primary aim is to be true to your valid beliefs and needs, even if the narcissist cannot recognize them—or you. You do not need that person's permission or agreement to remain firm in your resolve to uphold truth. While you might never find the cooperation you desire, that doesn't mean you have to abandon your principles or resort to the more negative ways of expressing anger. Assertiveness can be your way of indicating that you will not succumb to that person's manipulative demands.

For instance, Josh once fumed when he received a letter from Carrie detailing how he owed her money. Her demands were unfounded, and he knew he had been fair in all aspects of their finances. "What good does it do when I try to talk sense to her?" he asked. "She'll only use it as an opportunity to attack."

"Keep in mind," I mentioned, "that it is not your goal to extract good will from her. Instead, just stand your ground and maintain respect for yourself and for her." In the past Josh would have become drawn into a bitter argument about the falseness of her claims, but this time he chose a different path. "I've already handled that financial matter appropriately," he told her. "There is nothing further to discuss." When she launched into her usual blame, he calmly replied, "I realize our perspectives differ, but I am satisfied that I am handling this reasonably." Her continued efforts to engage him in an argument went nowhere. Even though they did not come to an agreement, his anger did not escalate as it would have in the past.

Josh's anger did not "work" in the sense that Carrie changed her mind and said nice things about his money management skills, but that did not have to be his objective. He held his ground while speaking the truth in a firm and fair manner, and that was enough.

I explained to him that he need not make the common mistake of letting satisfaction hinge on her response. She would undoubtedly be as self-absorbed as ever, but that was not Josh's problem to solve. A pleasant response from her would have been nice, but it was not essential to him being appropriate.

The thing to keep in mind here is that you never want to take your cues about managing your anger from a narcissist. Instead, you need to take a different path, one that allows you to stand up for your convictions and that fully recognizes that the narcissist will probably never respond positively. Expect the narcissist to try to make you feel guilty or weaken your resolve, but go into your interactions determined to stick to what you know is right, despite the predictable protests. There's no need to plead or justify yourself; that only draws you into a power play that you will inevitably lose.

Josh summarized his challenge in learning to use assertiveness constructively. "In the past, when Carrie would argue with me about my beliefs, I received it as an invitation to convince her that she was wrong and I was right. But if I'm hearing you correctly, it is not my job to convince her of anything. As long as I am being fair and dignified, then I have done my best, and I don't have to have her blessing as I stay the course."

"That's exactly right," I remarked. "It means that you are basing your emotional expressions on sound thinking, not on the desire to conquer. She might remain angry, but I'm making the assumption that you will be much less volatile once you let go of the illusion that you can rearrange her responses to you."

### 5. Releasing Anger

While an assertive approach to expressing anger can keep you out of prolonged power struggles, you still might not avoid tension and feelings of frustration altogether. Narcissists remain in an adversarial mode, continuing to try to provoke your anger. When you've been assertive, and there is nothing more that you can say or do to generate good will, you then can choose to release your anger. Successfully releasing your anger means that you will need to accept the unlikelihood that the other person will incorporate any new *insights from you*, no matter how cleanly you approach him or her. You might be at an emotional impasse, or it might be that the event that triggered the anger is finished. Either way, once you see the situation as it really is, you can decide not to cling to your anger.

Anger can be released through the following practices:

- Being willing to forgive
- Ceasing efforts to convince and moving on to other pursuits
- Showing tolerance for others' flaws and weaknesses
- Accepting that you are limited in gaining your way in every dispute
- Releasing the other person to God and renouncing yourself as the final judge
- Living with the lack of closure in emotional disputes
- Prioritizing goodness over vindication
- Knowing when not to press an issue; choosing battles carefully

Releasing anger will keep you out of emotional competitions with the narcissist and allow you to become healthier. You will undoubtedly be on your own in your efforts to release your anger, and you might very well struggle with feelings that the situation is unfair. Yet, ultimately you can stop insisting upon fairness and make a commitment to emotional stability.

Josh admitted, "When Carrie and I divorced, I assumed that I would no longer be bombarded by her irrational ways, but that hasn't proven to be the case. We don't disagree as much as we did when we lived under the same roof, but as long as we have to coordinate the needs of two kids, we will still have issues. I can't count the times when I have questioned why she can't be reasonable instead of being so selfish. I'm getting to the point, though, of accepting that I just need to quit asking that question and do the best I can under the circumstances. I'm the kind of person who likes closure, so accepting her irrationality is unnatural, but I'm also realizing that if I fixate on the need to change her, I'll remain stuck in some very sour emotions." Josh acknowledged that he would never fully understand Carrie's personality, yet he was learning that he did not have to understand her in order to manage his anger appropriately. They were two separate issues.

Josh was catching on to the idea that he could stop waiting for Carrie to cooperate with him so he could stop feeling so angry, but he wanted to be certain that in choosing to release anger he was not just suppressing his emotions. He once asked me, "How does the releasing of anger differ from the suppression of anger? Am I just storing my difficult emotions for some later expressions?"

I responded, "That's a good question, because it forces you to become honest about your real motives. If indeed you are suppressing the emotion, it will come back later in some ugly form; that would indicate that your efforts to address your anger were little more than window dressing. For instance, people who suppress anger often experience depression or struggle with chronic disillusionment. They are hardly ever at true peace. When you suppress anger, you are applying a phony front and are just trying to do damage control. Truly releasing anger, however, involves some serious soul-searching for your true priorities. It forces you to ponder if you genuinely believe, for instance, in the goodness of forgiveness or kindness or tolerance. As you weigh the benefits of these priorities, you can honestly conclude that while you have reasons to continue feeling angry, you would rather make other choices. You are then operating not as a phony but as one who understands that he has a mission in life to accomplish, regardless of how Carrie behaves."

Josh had a chance to practice releasing anger when he learned that Carrie had spoken disparaging words about him to a family member. He immediately reexperienced old feelings of bitterness as he questioned why there seemed to be no end to her slanderous words. He wanted to phone her and tell her exactly how agitated he felt, but remembering our discussions, he paused to reflect. Carrie had never shown much inclination to consider his feelings or perspectives, especially since they divorced, and there was an extremely low probability that an angry phone call about this latest incident would generate new results. He decided that this would be a good time to release his anger, so he chose to accept the truth that she was a troubled person who would probably continue to speak venomously about him in the future. He did not like the prospect of knowing that she would remain an adversary, yet there was little he could do to change that fact. Accepting Carrie's nature allowed him to begin separating from bitter feelings that would ultimately be his downfall. He wanted to live in confidence and peace, even when it meant accepting that she would continue to scorn him.

Releasing anger demonstrates that you have committed to healthy living. While the narcissist would like nothing more than to jerk your emotional chains, you don't have to play along. You can let go of the fantasy that you will ever get that person's blessing or cooperation. Such a decision is not made with a spirit of defeat or harshness; rather, it is an acknowledgment of the truth of your situation and that person's character.

Narcissists love knowing that they can keep you trapped in emotional turmoil, no matter what efforts you make toward greater health. Let them play their games, and recognize that you can choose not to play—to not even enter the playing field in the first place. While their behaviors are not entirely irrelevant to your emotional stability, neither are they central to it.

To manage your anger effectively you must come to peace with yourself and not let fear and mistrust direct your thoughts and behaviors. In the next chapter, we will explore how you can learn to sidestep the fear and defensiveness that comes upon you as you continue to interact with the narcissist.

## Chapter Seven

# Removing Fear from the Equation

Austin was a bright and eager recent college graduate trying to succeed as a medical equipment sales representative. In his previous jobs he had established a reputation as someone who was reliable, self-motivated, and confident.

Just a few months into his new job, he came to see me because he was experiencing such anxiety that he wanted to figure out why he was struggling and what he could do about it. As he spoke with me about his circumstances, he explained how baffled he felt with his sales supervisor. "I never get the same message from him two days in a row," he said. "Mr. Spenser likes to motivate by intimidation, and he's constantly finding fault in anything I do. One day he'll give me assignments, then after I do them exactly as he instructs, he scolds me and tells me to do them differently. He's constantly in a foul mood, and I hate being around him. All other aspects of my job are good. I like my co-workers, the pay is decent, and I feel good about our product. I just can't stand my boss."

To make matters worse, Austin's boss reminded him of his very overwhelming father. Although they were no longer in daily contact, on the occasions when Austin and his dad were together, and his father started to make demands on him and treat him like a child, his anxiety would surface again. "My dad verbally wears people out," Austin explained. "He's never wrong, and he seems oblivious to the fact that family members have needs and feelings that should be respected. I've given up trying to talk with him about anything of substance, because it will lead to some sort of lecture."

When interacting with either his dad or Mr. Spenser, Austin said he often found his heart beating rapidly and felt himself becoming cautious and guarded. "I wish I wouldn't lose my cool when I am with each of them," he said, "because I know that I shouldn't let their problems affect me so powerfully. Each in his own way can be so condescending and bull-headed that I just can't stand being around them. Neither of them shows respect for my feelings, and that bothers me greatly. And to top it off, there is no indication that either recognizes that there is a problem."

Narcissists have an uncanny knack for generating doubt and uncertainty in the people closest to them. Even those of us who are normally confident begin to waffle in the face of a narcissist's persistently invalidating communication. As part of their quest to feel special, narcissists will be unapologetically demanding, stubborn, or self-seeking in their responses. When questioned, they bolster their positions by discrediting anyone else's preferences or points of view. Often they are skilled debaters, or if they sense that they cannot out-reason their opponent, they resort to emotional outbursts, accusations, or demands. Only their needs matter, so if they have to undermine others' confidence in order to get their way, they will not hesitate to do so.

As we saw in Chapter Six, anger is the first and most observable response to the narcissist's selfish behavior, yet when frustration and tension linger, anger is likely to become an extension of the deeper problem of fear. When the other person simmers with agitation and annoyance, that's evidence that he or she is feeling threatened. Fear and frustration can be a way of saying to the narcissist, "I can't believe you are doing this to me! How can I possibly move forward if you continue being so unreasonable? This is too much for me to handle. I feel terribly inadequate right now."

We often stereotype fear by assuming that it is accompanied by a terrified reaction or horrified dread; if those extreme reactions are missing, we can falsely assume that we're not afraid. While fear can certainly include strong feelings of fright or panic, it can also manifest as apprehension, anxiety, self-doubt, hesitation, or paralysis.

Any time you act more self-protectively than the circumstance warrants, you can be assured that fear has taken control. Fear leads to many forms of defense that attempt to fend off unwanted intrusions. And given the aggressiveness and intrusiveness of most narcissists, it's a predictable reaction to their behavior.

Austin was not the only one who had trouble with his boss and his father; both men had reputations of being problematic and insensitive—both were clearly narcissistic. In helping Austin, I wanted him to understand that, although his reactions were normal, he did not have to remain permanently paralyzed by his interactions with these men. Fear did not have to be a central feature in his responses.

## The Forms of Fear

The first step for anyone dealing with fearful responses to a narcissist is to figure out what forms it is taking. Fear can manifest itself in many ways:

- Feeling the need to rationalize or justify your decisions
- Being reluctant to be as assertive as you need to be
- Agreeing, even though you don't really agree, because it temporarily puts an end to the conflict
- Feeling that resistance is so futile you suppress your emotions
- Repeating the same words again and again even though you have no confidence you are being listened to
- Avoiding the other person even if you have to alter your activities unnaturally
- Telling lies or leaving out essential information as a means of avoiding conflict
- Working too hard to gain the other person's approval or to prove a point
- Complaining about the antagonist to others rather than confronting the antagonist

- Allowing yourself to be mistreated without standing up for your legitimate needs
- Second-guessing your preferences and letting your antagonist talk you out of decisions you know are right

As Austin and I identified numerous ways fear had gained a foothold in his personality, he admitted that he often altered his behaviors to appease others. It bothered him, because he was not true to his real beliefs. As an example, he explained, "If I have an especially good day of sales, Mr. Spenser can still find fault with my work. I really feel he has an unusual need to be superior, and even though he benefits from my success, he just cannot tolerate the thought that anyone else should receive praise. He'll tell me to change the ways I approach certain clients, not because I should be doing things differently but because he wants to show he is still the boss. I know I should stand up to him and tell him that I am comfortable with the ways I handle my accounts, but I don't. I've learned from my colleagues that I won't be fired as long as I am doing my job adequately, yet I still let the man lord it over me because I don't want to hassle with his crummy moods."

As Austin considered how easily he cowered to Mr. Spenser's abrasiveness, he recognized that his behavior consistently made him anxious. That anxiety became an increasingly prominent trait even when he was not really being threatened. He was slowly losing confidence as he continued to ignore his fearful responses.

As you try to make sense of the fear you're feeling in your interactions with the narcissist in your life, keep in mind that it doesn't come out of nowhere. There are several factors to consider. Let's identify some of them here.

### Doomed to Repeat History

When people such as Austin allow narcissists to dominate through fear, they usually have had experiences in their lives that predispose them to buckle under pressure. Most commonly, they were not taught to believe in the legitimacy of their own feelings or perceptions; instead they were told that they were wrong (or that other people were more right). Most recall how influential people in their lives responded to their struggles in ways that created doubt rather than confidence and affirmation.

Developing children need to learn that their perceptions are usually valid, just as they need careful guidance to learn how to get along with those around them. Children might be selfish in their insistence on their way, but that does not mean they are entirely off base. Parents and other authorities can teach children to have confidence in their decisions and coach them in communicating their feelings more appropriately. For instance, if a nine-year-old child has a conflict with a sibling, it is common for the parent to say something like, "You're going to have to learn to get along better than that. I'm not going to tolerate arguing!" In that situation, the child legitimately feels frustrated; when the parent demeans those feelings, the child's confidence is undermined. Instead, the parent could say something like, "It sounds like you had some reasonable concerns that your sister didn't want to consider. Let's figure out how you could keep your beliefs while at the same time being less argumentative. How do you suppose that would work?" The first approach invalidates, while the second approach validates and encourages the child to look at other alternatives. Parents have to be very patient and repeat themselves often to use such a validating approach. Since many families have a short supply of patience, children can feel their emotions and needs are not appreciated and fear can begin to ripple through the rest of their lives. Narcissists are naturally inclined to be overly self-protective, so when they are in conflict with others, they tend to go on the attack. If you're someone who has a history of feeling less than confident when you encounter conflict, you can feel threatened and overpowered—and thus vulnerable to manipulation.

## Exaggerated Defenses

While it is natural for people such as Austin to defend themselves when others are excessively critical or pushy, when someone has an inclination toward fear, his or her defenses are likely to be more easily activated than necessary. Already prone to questioning their core competence, these people can develop elaborate means of self-protection.

Sometimes they use unnecessary rationalization or justification, while at other times they tell "white lies" to create a more favorable impression. They might be evasive, trying to deny or avoid the reality of the situation. When confronted, they are apt to stop listening for fear that the other person will interpret listening as agreement. The irony of these responses (all of which indicate that the person has low self-confidence) is that they only empower narcissists to continue their offensive behavior.

### Exaggerated Responsibility

Narcissists always feel affirmed when they can convince others to also become impressed with their power and special status. That is why they are so pushy about communicating their needs and why they want to convince others that they are owed favored treatment. They feel they must be right so they can remain superior, and that kind of thinking feeds their insensitivity, stubbornness, and rigidity toward others. Fearful people such as Austin, who have spent a lot of time around narcissists, allow themselves to be duped into thinking it is their responsibility to keep narcissists feeling calm or acting reasonable. As they witness narcissists being overbearing or angry, they might think, "What should I do now to keep this problem from becoming worse?" They try to appease by saying whatever the narcissist wants to hear in order to minimize further conflict. They might alter their plans to create a false sense of peace. Perhaps they try to argue for the purpose of forcing change. In all of these tactics, they illustrate that they have little confidence that their own priorities and perceptions are reasonable. By trying too hard to make things right, they unwittingly invite increasing amounts of abuse.

### Idealistic Assumptions

In Chapter One, we talked about how narcissists are not in touch with reality. So distorted is their sense of uniqueness that they can-

not accept the truth that they don't deserve any more favored treatment than anyone else. And that means they don't believe they
should have to live with the same limits or accountability as others.

Even though fearful partners of narcissists might be more in
touch with reality, they too can suffer an idealism that keeps them
from drawing firm boundary lines in the relationship. For instance,
it is common for partners to make excuses for narcissists with statements such as these:

- "He's just having a bad day."
- "If I can stay in a good mood, maybe she will snap out of it."
- "If I don't say anything to him about my hurt feelings, maybe
  he will eventually realize that he's being a little too stubborn."
- "I know he's frequently in a bad mood, but really, he's just a
  nice guy."
- "Surely this behavior won't go on indefinitely."
- "If I continue to be agreeable, I can eventually gain his
  cooperation."

The more we tolerate the narcissist's destructive behavior, the more
our idealistic thinking clouds our good judgment. The less willing
we are to accept the truth that narcissists care little beyond themselves, we might find ourselves clinging to the hope that they will
change or that the problems with the narcissist are not as severe as
they really are. Fear prevents us from facing the fact that narcissism
is a problem that requires strong resolve. We might not be out of
touch with reality in the same way narcissists are, yet we are not
being honest about the problems that create uncomfortable exchanges.

### Minimized Personal Needs

Fearful people do not want to believe their problems are as serious as they really are, because that could make them emotionally
vulnerable—and that vulnerability could provoke an unpleasant

response from the narcissist. Since fearful people have trained themselves to avoid uncomfortable emotions, it can seem easier to minimize the extent of the difficulties they face. They become too willing to ignore the legitimacy of their own personal needs.

For instance, the wife of a narcissist might want to discuss a scheduling conflict with her husband, but as she anticipates his combative response, she might tell herself that she doesn't really need to go to the event that would cause the conflict. Likewise, a co-worker might want to pursue ideas that might not meet the narcissist's approval and so will talk himself out of pursuing his ideas because he doesn't want a fight. He might rationalize his action as a display of team spirit, when in fact his doubt about his own ideas leads him to avoid the interaction altogether.

## Setting Fear Aside

If you're a fearful person, your feelings of apprehension in dealing with a narcissist can be quite reasonable. Your perception is correct: the narcissist will not want to give priority to your needs or ideas (or anyone else's) and will try to manipulate and belittle you so that you retreat from whatever you had resolved to do. To find a more productive way of managing the narcissist, you will need to find another primary response besides fear. As I talked with Austin about the fear that lay beneath his anxiety, he admitted that his confidence could quickly melt when faced with chiding from either Mr. Spenser or his dad. "I hate it when someone so routinely dismisses me as some inconsequential fool. I know I'm a rookie at work, but that doesn't mean that I bring nothing good to the table. I'm definitely pulling my weight, and I'm ahead of the learning curve for the job I'm doing, but to listen to my boss, you would think I just fell off the turnip truck."

I applauded him for believing in his skills, then I suggested that it might be time for Austin to show Mr. Spenser that he deserved to be reckoned with as an adult, not some underage schoolboy. Austin looked pale as he replied tentatively. "There have been times when

I wanted to tell him that I am on top of my projects, and that I intend to follow my own good judgment, but I haven't gotten up the nerve to do so." As we talked further, he also admitted that there were incidents when he seethed from his father's continuing belittlement, but he never indicated that he would no longer tolerate that treatment either. Austin was stuck in a pattern that would be harder and harder to break if he chose to maintain the status quo.

Austin and I agreed that it was time to face his fears and to respond differently to the narcissism of his boss and his dad. He began realizing that if he allowed himself to be steamrollered by their pomposity, his anxiety would only deepen. He also recognized that it made no sense to let his emotional stability be so powerfully controlled by men who were unwilling to address their own personality deficiencies. The primary issue I wanted him to examine was inner trust.

### Developing Inner Trust

The opposite of fear is trust. We develop fearful responses because we have been exposed to messages and circumstances that seem untrustworthy, and our natural reaction is self-protection. Often, fear can be reasonable; those who mistreat us can indeed be quite menacing or threatening. For instance, I did not fault Austin for feeling fearful when Mr. Spenser spoke threatening words toward him—he was Austin's boss. Austin's fear alerted him, appropriately so, to be wary of responding in a way that would only worsen the problem.

But Austin doesn't have to be stuck in his fearful state. He can learn to interact with others, even narcissists, without being paralyzed by mistrust. Though he might never come to trust his antagonists, he can learn to trust himself. And that is how he can start to break fear's hold on his personality.

I wanted Austin to learn to look inward rather than outward as he struggled with fear, so I asked him, "When Mr. Spenser treats you in a condescending manner, what valid thoughts are running through your mind?"

He paused a moment, then replied, "I'm usually thinking that I don't deserve the garbage he is dishing out. I want to be respected."

"Let me get this straight," I said. "He might be in the midst of a nasty tirade, or he might be highly critical of you, and you immediately think that you deserve better than that. Am I hearing you correctly?" He nodded in agreement. Then I asked, "So at that point, how is your behavior affected by such thinking?"

Once again Austin paused, then he said, "I shut down. I don't take my thoughts of self-respect any further."

"That," I pointed out, "is when you allow your fear to run with you instead of trusting your own valid notions. Even though you have a reasonable desire for dignity and respect at that moment, you place your trust in his pronouncements. His message belittles you, and your acquiescence indicates that you agree with his assessment of you. Is that your real intention?"

Austin grinned as he began recognizing where I was going. "No, I don't agree with his low assessment of me," he said, "and furthermore I don't want to give the impression that it's okay for him to continue his harassment."

"It sounds to me, then, that you will need to behave in a manner that shows that you trust in a separate version of truth: your version. Before your behavior can be different, though, you will need to be convinced that your self-assessment is indeed valid, no matter what Mr. Spenser says."

Like Austin, your fear of others is directly proportional to your unwillingness to trust your own legitimate beliefs about yourself. The moment you feel afraid of a narcissist's behavior, you are at a fork in the road. You can choose to give in to the fear as you tell yourself that you cannot possibly stand up to the narcissist, or you can choose to trust in your own instincts and speak or act as you know is best, regardless of the narcissist's lack of approval. When you choose to trust yourself, you take fear out of the driver's seat and signal that you are not intimidated by the narcissist's chest thumping.

The next day after Austin and I began discussing the possibility of trusting himself more, he had an all-too-familiar encounter with his dad regarding a financial matter. When Austin told his father that he had decided to purchase a new car, his dad immediately scorned the decision. In a harsh and condescending tone of voice he said, "That would be a stupid thing to do, son, because you know that you can't afford it. Besides, your current car does what you need it to do. Don't go making one of your dumb mistakes." Austin knew his budget had room for the purchase and that his old car was showing major signs of wear and tear. He believed he was making a reasonable and informed decision. In the past, he would have become quite defensive and flustered in an attempt to justify his thinking. This time, however, he remembered that he was at a fork in the road and that he could choose to follow his own trustworthy instinct, with or without his dad's blessing. So he replied, "I've given this decision plenty of thought, and it makes sense to me. I'll be picking up my new car tomorrow." When his dad continued his tongue lashing, Austin listened, then softly repeated, "My decision still makes good sense, and I'll still be picking up the car tomorrow." No defense. No cowering. No agonizing. It was time to act like an unafraid adult, and to do so, he had to believe in his own validity. The fact that his dad would not validate him was irrelevant. Austin was learning that he could never expect a narcissist to set aside his selfish notions, and he was realizing how foolhardy it was to try to force agreement with one who was chronically blinded by his own biases.

You can display trust in yourself in a number of ways:

- A narcissistic husband can scold his wife for the way she disciplines their child. Knowing she was making the wisest decision under the circumstances, she can say, "I'm satisfied that I did the right thing." When he continues berating her, she can reiterate, "I did what I believed to be best." Nothing more needs to be said.

- As a woman makes social plans, her sister tries to manipulate her into changing those plans. This is an ongoing part of the sister's efforts to control her, so the woman stays with her original plans, feeling no need to justify her decision.

- A father physically and verbally abused his son for years, and now the son is choosing to distance himself from the dad, who shows no signs of remorse. When he receives word that his father wants to talk with him about his changing priorities, he has no confidence that the discussion will be anything other than a chance to try to badger him into submission. He declines to meet and stays the course.

There is a high probability that the narcissist will not understand or agree with your decision to trust in your own instincts, but remember that such a reaction is only to be expected. They do not empathize with feelings or needs that do not suit their purposes, so they naturally seek to squelch what they do not like. Their responses are not a referendum on your core value, only more manifestations of how central self-absorption is to the narcissistic pattern.

### Inner Trust and Unbroken Resolve

I was fortunate to work with Austin while he was still young enough to make adjustments that could serve him well for years, even decades. Many of the people I see, though, do not come to terms with their fears until much later in life, so they have more emotional baggage to unload. Even though change can require unnatural shifts in thought and behavior, it can still happen. If nothing else, your misery can prompt you to stop doing business as usual. The emotional fallout from unsuccessful interactions with self-absorbed people can signal that it is time to adjust.

As you learn to anchor yourself more deeply in self-trust, I'd like to offer you four suggestions for attitudinal and behavioral changes that can significantly shift your responses to narcissism.

**1. Do Not Be Threatened by the Narcissist's Wrong Perceptions.** In a perfect world, you would be able to speak and act with the assurance that others perceive your ideas and feelings correctly. At the very least, you would want to know that if others do not understand you fully, they would still show you respect and dignity as they tried to build bridges of understanding. Perhaps you actually have relationships that approach such a standard—but none of those will be with a narcissist.

Because narcissists cannot tolerate the thought that their perceptions are wrong or misguided, they will often try to make you think that you are the one in the wrong. Sometimes their insistence upon perfect correctness is so exaggerated that it borders on the absurd, but they will stop at nothing to foist their opinions on you, even if it means obliterating you and your perceptions. If you don't agree with them, they'll see that as an invitation to become even more stubborn or persuasive. When Mr. Spenser corrected Austin on how he should manage an account, Austin tried to explain what he was doing, providing information that his boss had overlooked. Yet Mr. Spenser lectured him as if he had not even heard Austin. Likewise, if Austin explained a decision to his father, he was likely to be told, "You don't know what you are talking about."

In response, Austin might be tempted to argue with his father or Mr. Spenser, but that is futile. Instead, he can choose to stand his ground. I explained to Austin, "There is no need to defend that which needs no defense. For instance, if Mr. Spenser belittles your ideas, that is his prerogative, yet it does not mean that you need to buckle under the pressure. You can listen to his thoughts, and if you are confident that your ideas still make sense, you can say something like, 'I'll certainly listen to your perspective while I will still consider my own ideas too.' You don't have to be intimidated by his hard-headedness. There is a good chance that he would be this way no matter who he is talking to."

It is not pleasant or comfortable when a narcissist summarily dismisses your feelings and thoughts, yet your discomfort need not become the beginning point for appeasement. Drop the wish for the narcissist to change. It is not likely to happen. Instead, look inward and determine if you are operating with reasonable notions and impressions. If you are, you can proceed in the confidence that the narcissist's lack of understanding does not negate your trust in yourself.

Your confident mindset can override the narcissist's invalidating comments or actions.

**2. Stop Justifying Your Choices.** Narcissists have learned that they can win personal battles if they draw others into conversations of one-upmanship. As they invite others to clarify their thoughts, narcissists will seek faults in the logic and then use those faults as an excuse for not cooperating. Simply put, you cannot win an argument with a narcissist. As I talked with Austin about the futility of arguing with a narcissist, he sighed as he said, "When I was still living at home, I just gave up trying to talk with my dad about anything of substance. My mother and sister were constantly at odds with him, and he would reduce one of them to tears on a regular basis. He and my mother could argue for hours about trivia, and it always ended with her feeling very upset."

"When you would witness those exchanges, what forms of communication seemed to stand out?" I asked this question because I suspected strong parallels between Austin's father's treatment of his wife and his son.

"Dad was always on the attack," he replied. "My mother could hardly ever make a point without him explaining why she was wrong. She would keep the argument alive by trying to make him understand that he should listen to her. Of course, she virtually never got through to him, but it didn't stop her from trying." Austin went on to explain that his parents would go round and round with very little being solved.

"I'm sure you have had the same feeling of exasperation that your mother did," I mentioned. Austin was wide-eyed as he nodded his head in agreement. "Let's learn from your observations and conclude that no matter how airtight your arguments are, there is a low likelihood that you will force your dad to see what he does not want to see. Would that be a fair assumption?" Again Austin nodded.

"When you disagree with someone such as your dad, it is fair for you to attempt to explain once why you have chosen to think and act as you do. But if you receive little more than a verbal attack, then you can stop trying to enlighten him. There is no need to engage in an unproductive battle."

Austin was following my reasoning, yet he asked a common question. "But what am I going to do, knowing that he won't agree or cooperate?"

"Well, you certainly do not have to shake in fear. I'll admit that life would be a lot easier if you could somehow gain his understanding, but given his long uncooperative history, I doubt that you will ever be able to say the right thing to cause him to respect your words. That being the case, leave him alone. You can proceed without his understanding or approval."

Do my comments to Austin seem cold to you? In fact, they are more realistic than cold (especially because the narcissist is impervious to changes in the emotional temperature). The possibility that you'll be able to change the narcissist or that he or she will listen to you is nil. As you stop trying to engage and justify, you show that you do not view the relationship as a competition for who has superior ideas.

**3. Go Beyond Talk and Take Action Toward Change.** Partners of narcissists do a lot of talking about responding in more confident ways, but they do not always follow up their talk with decisive action, which is the key to real change. Once you determine that the narcissist's offensiveness is not threatening, and your ideas are legitimate, you can choose to act on your own good judgment. The narcissist might not think you have good judgment, but the narcissist is not God. You do not have to be guided by his or her pronouncements. When you abandon your desire to win over the narcissist, you can stand firmly in your self-respect and rely on your good decisions.

Austin reflected, "It's sad to say, but both Mr. Spencer and my father are bullies who are not guided by a strong conscience. It is a relief to think that I can unhook from their moods and go my own way, with or without their approval. I guess you are trying to teach me that I should quit worrying so much about their selfishness and focus more on my own good traits." I nodded my head and mentioned that too much attention to their negative traits would detract from his ability to find comfort in his own positive traits.

I then told Austin, "Whether you realize it or not, you are always sending cues to others that tell them what you believe about yourself. This is called *covert communication*. For instance, if you cower too readily when someone is pushy, you covertly communicate, 'Go ahead and take advantage of my good nature; you'll probably get away with it.' Likewise, if you work too hard to rationalize your decisions, you covertly indicate, 'I'm feeling insecure about my reasoning, and I am not likely to stand my ground if you keep pushing your agenda.' Is that what you really want to convey?"

Austin shook his head, and then I said, "By suggesting that you act decisively, I am not encouraging you to become aggressive or inappropriately stubborn. I am suggesting that you let your covert communication exude confidence. You are a decent person with solid work habits and relationship goals. There is no reason for you to set aside your preferred way of living just because these self-centered people in your life behave the way they do."

**4. Forget About Generating Good Will.** When people give in to fear, they usually believe that they must keep others feeling good about their interactions. Fearful people think, "Oh no, I can't handle it if you continue to have bad feelings. I must do all within my power to make things right." While it is good to want peace and harmony, it is necessary to remember that narcissists are much more concerned about getting their way than about harmony. When they sense that you are working overtime to maintain good feelings, they will interpret that behavior as an invitation to continue in their controlling ways.

Austin once told me about a co-worker who seemed to have few problems with Mr. Spenser's overbearing managerial style. When he asked the colleague about her approach toward their boss, she said, "When I first joined the company, he tried the same intimidation approach on me. I knew that I was a good producer, and

I immediately recognized that any angry meltdown he experienced was his problem, not mine. I would listen to his input, but at the same time I gave myself permission to proceed with my work as I deemed appropriate. The bottom line is that I get results, and my solid work ethic speaks for itself. I don't need to change my behavior just to get some egomaniac off my back." As she spoke, she was not haughty, just confident.

Austin too could fall back on his good work ethic. Though he would have liked more good will between him and Mr. Spenser, he was learning that his boss was a troubled man who was not likely to change. Austin had not been trained as a youth to act in a self-trusting manner, but now as an adult he could reorient his beliefs, acknowledging that it was good to act upon his positive traits—regardless of what Mr. Spenser would think about him.

As you, like Austin, consider how to minimize the fear factor in your interactions with a narcissist, be willing to focus less on the other person's flawed reasoning and more on your own inner character. As you recognize the good within, you can conclude that the narcissist's inability to appreciate you is unfortunate but not fatal.

*Chapter Eight*

# Committing to Humility

As part of my work, I often speak at conferences all over the United States. Since I have lived most of my life in Texas or Georgia, I speak with a distinct Southern accent, so I am amused when I go to places like New Jersey or Michigan and encounter people who tease me about the way I pronounce words. I am quick to point out that while my way of speaking might strike them as odd, to me they are the ones who sound strange.

I have a Southern accent not because I'm putting it on to sound a certain way. It's the way I've spoken and heard others speak my whole life. I just absorbed my accent, so that it's a natural and permanent part of me. In much the same way, when you have ongoing interactions with narcissists, whether you realize it or not, you can become vulnerable to thinking and behaving just like them. Selfish behavior in one person breeds selfish behavior in another. Controlling initiatives generate controlling responses. Poor listening is often met with poor listening. Narcissists have a way of turning normal conversations into a battle for power and influence, so it's common for those trying to relate to them to respond in kind.

Beneath the behaviors and attitudes associated with narcissism there is an underlying pride. Narcissists are so driven by the hunger to feed their egotistical cravings that they cannot factor in the needs and feelings of those around them. Their pride blinds them from recognizing that others too have legitimate issues.

It is easy for us to point an accusing finger at narcissists and say, "That person is so selfish that he proves just how troubled he really is." All the while, we might be dismissing how willingly we can become drawn into a self-centered pattern of behavior. Part of the task of those who must deal with narcissists is to recognize and understand the nature of pride so we can avoid becoming ensnared by the very traits we dislike so much in them.

## Positive Pride, Negative Pride

None of us is without pride, but as an emotion we can experience it either positively or negatively. With positive pride, we feel a sense of pleasure with ourselves. It involves feelings of personal satisfaction, inner peace, and contentment with the way things are. When people are expressing pride in their children, in their country, or in a job well done, those are indications that they have surveyed their circumstances and found them to be rewarding. Positive pride can certainly go a long way in generating feelings of true contentment.

The negative form of pride, however, taints the human spirit by excessively feeding our egotistical yearnings, cravings, preferences, and desires, which are typical narcissistic tendencies. Negative pride expresses itself as the need for control and the inability to account for the needs of others. Negative pride grows out of our inborn sin nature and is the fundamental ingredient that influences every other negative trait in the human personality. It is that pervasive.

We see negative pride in all kinds of strongly offensive behaviors. It is pride, for instance, that compels individuals to be loud and obnoxious, argumentative, brash, rude, insulting, and openly rebellious. It is at the heart of bullying or demanding behavior, sharp criticism, sarcasm, intimidation, threats, false accusations, and condescending communications. Those displaying these openly disrespectful behaviors are so consumed with their personal agenda that they make little effort to show consideration toward others.

All negative pride is not quite as obviously harmful. It might just be annoying or problematic when it manifests as defensiveness, fretting, worrying, impatience, persistent interruption, and intrusiveness. It might also turn up when people attempt to induce false guilt in others, dominate conversations, or attempt to force their opinions. It is evidenced in gossiping, lying, whining, griping, foul language, disrespect, jealousy, and stubbornness. Not all negative pride is so aggressive. It might also show up in passive ways, as when people withdraw or refuse to speak, use silence as punishment, refuse to exert themselves, or procrastinate. It is also associated with another whole range of behaviors like unreliability, chronic forgetfulness, smugness, secretiveness, quitting, ignoring others, refusing to follow directions, indulging lust, giving half-hearted efforts, sullenness, spaciness, and arrogance.

Pride is an insidious characteristic that can worm its way into every part of the personality, influencing us to shun responsibilities of every variety. Furthermore, no individual is so spiritually and emotionally balanced that he or she will never struggle with this character defect. Each of us has struggled to tame selfishness from the earliest stages of life, and no one can claim to have conquered it completely. We might differ in the amount of pride we manifest, but no one can claim complete immunity from it.

As I counsel with individuals trying to make sense of others' narcissistic behavior, I emphasize that they are likely to feel woefully inadequate in their ability to motivate change. Rather than spinning their wheels in ongoing attempts to reform those who will not be reformed, I explain that they can expend their emotional energies more successfully if they focus on their own tendencies toward emotional imbalance. They, like all of us, need to admit that others' difficult behavior might bring out the worst in them, but that is something they can manage.

Despite the common sense of this kind of advice, it's not easy to curb our own prideful impulses when faced with a narcissist's intense self-absorption. Recall Cindy, introduced in Chapter One as a divorcing woman trying to come to terms with the pain that her soon-to-be ex-husband, Martin, caused her. Cindy was a naturally friendly woman who had felt her confidence being whittled away by Martin's repeated criticisms and accusations, his need to dominate, and his condescending and manipulative spirit. No matter how many good traits she showed, he could readily find fault with her. Martin was bossy and self-righteous. When they experienced relationship problems, it had to be her fault, because he was virtually never wrong (or so he assumed).

As the weeks and months passed, Cindy struggled to find peace in her new life away from Martin. They had a son, Preston, who was a freshman in college, and a daughter, Christie, who was a sophomore in high school. This meant that Cindy still had to coordinate activities with Martin, and rarely was he cooperative or pleasant. "He is the world's most argumentative man," she told me. "If I tell him about one of Christie's events, he will point out how I'm not managing her schedule correctly, or he'll criticize me because he feels she is spending too much money. He seems to look for excuses to make our lives miserable. He feels very free to correct or scold me and our kids."

I had noticed that Cindy seemed to cling to pessimistic thoughts, so I pointed this out. I told her that I could understand that she would like to have a much different style of communication with Martin, but we'd have to concede that it is not likely that he will engage with her in a cordial manner. I reminded her that this was simply not in his nature. She nodded reluctantly as I continued. "As I hear you describing your exchanges with him, I am concerned that your animosity is eating away at your ability to remain composed. You seem to be tied up in knots every time you encounter him."

"I dread every exchange I have with him," she admitted, "because there is such a high probability that he will be antagonistic. If he doesn't get his way, he turns into a bully. I hate having to talk with him!" She then described how she was consistently agitated and defensive in most interactions with him.

I challenged her to examine how easily she fell into maladaptive patterns whenever she was in Martin's presence. "Cindy, it's normal that you would feel frustrated by Martin's cranky disposition, yet I'd like you to consider how you have inadvertently allowed yourself to become selfish even as you protest his selfish behavior."

She knew that there was a ring of truth to what I was saying, but I could tell that she wanted further clarification. I explained, "When he speaks to you in a pushy, unbending tone of voice, that is evidence that he is so absorbed with his own agenda that he cannot accommodate a separate idea." She nodded in agreement as she quickly recalled the many times his mind was too closed to hear her needs. I continued, "When you argue back with him in a brash, forceful tone of voice, you are reenacting the very thing you dislike about him. Something's not right with that picture." We discussed how she had incorporated several of his bad communication habits. For example, he could interrupt easily as she spoke, but so did she. Likewise, Martin expressed his opinions strongly and persuasively, leaving no room for a separate perspective, so Cindy often responded in kind. Sometimes, Martin used sarcasm, a trait that Cindy abhorred. Yet she could recall numerous times when she too had been sarcastic.

As we listed several more ways in which she displayed some of the very traits she disliked in Martin, she began to understand that she had some real soul-searching to do if she were going to stop being chronically discouraged by her interactions with him. She showed real insight when she said, "I can see that I've been so consumed by his negative treatment of me that I've neglected my own personal growth. I hate to admit it, but in some ways, I can be just as dysfunctional as he is. Yuk!"

Cindy is not alone in the problem of responding to selfishness with selfishness. Because narcissists show so little regard for others' feelings, their partners rightly assume that they need to be proactive just to preserve themselves. However, because they too possess an inborn, sinful inclination to be selfish, they make the mistake of allowing self-preservation to turn into self-absorption as they cease to respond constructively and treat the other person disrespectfully. So consumed are they by their rights that they forget their responsibilities. To keep from responding to pride with pride, they need to focus on its opposite, humility.

## Humility Is Strength

Humility is the opposite of pride because it reflects a lack of self-preoccupation, a willingness to serve, an acknowledgment that we are limited in our ability to control other people and circumstances, and an understanding that we cannot demand favored treatment. Rather than responding to dysfunction with dysfunction or to evil with evil, we can determine that we will maintain our own goodness even when another person does not. This does not mean acquiescing passively to the narcissist's demands; it means being proactive in seeking reasonable treatment but doing so with a spirit of decency, without seeking to demean the other person. Humble people accept that life does not always play out as desired. By embracing humility, we illustrate that we do not want to play God, but we are willing to release the narcissist to the care of the real God.

Often when I introduce the topic of humility to people who, like Cindy, have struggled with very selfish people, they protest. "If I act humbly around a narcissist," they explain, "I'm only inviting that person to walk all over me." These people see humility as a trait that causes a person to be pleasant, but weak. Such a characterization could not be further from the truth.

While humble people indeed are not boisterous or arrogant, they are not pushovers, either. People who truly embody humility are quietly confident and are not prone to irrational outbursts; nor are they easily drawn into unhealthy scuffles. Humility grounds a person in the realization that life is not always fair, yet it can be manageable. Genuinely humble people are psychologically secure because they do not require others to dote on them, nor do they try to position themselves for favored treatment. Even as they lay down the wish to play God, they also choose not to allow another human to assume the position of a god over them.

Cindy told me of an incident with Martin that aroused her anger and defensiveness. He had promised Christie that he would buy some necessary items for a school social, but when the deadline came, he had not done as promised. Naturally, their daughter was frustrated and tense as she and Cindy scrambled at the last minute to make up for Martin's lapse. "This is so typical of Martin," she later conveyed to me. "He'll make grand promises, then he will renege with no apologies. Whenever I try to pin him down for an explanation, he can always come up with a good excuse, and amazingly it is somehow my fault. That's when I blow up and get drawn into arguments with him."

I asked Cindy to examine her response carefully. "At the moment you became angry, what was the valid message you were wishing to convey?"

She paused momentarily, then said, "I wanted him to be a man of his word. If he says he will do something, he needs to do it. Also, I wanted him to quit toying with my daughter's emotions." This made sense to me, and it showed that her anger was indeed legitimate.

My next question aimed at helping her see how her prideful spirit tainted her valid anger. After we discussed how her valid feelings had been derailed for several minutes, she began realizing that her craving for control had wormed its way into her communication with him. She admitted that she ultimately would not accept his irresponsibility toward her and their daughter. I explained, "It's like you are shouting, 'I can't believe he is doing this to *me*! Doesn't he know who I am?' Your sense of pride causes you to insist that he must give you correct treatment, and if he does not, you will pitch a fit. You seem to forget that he treats lots of other people the same way, meaning that his behavior is not really about you. Your fundamental belief is still solid, but pride can run with you in the sense that you turn his behavior into a referendum about you."

"Okay, I can see your point," she replied, "but what are my alternatives?"

"Consider responding to Martin with a mind of humility when he lies to you or when he is manipulative," I said. "In humility, you can begin with the recognition that his foul treatment says something about his character, not yours. That being the case, you will not be inclined to turn the problem into a discussion about you or your daughter."

Cindy interjected and asked, "Do you mean that I won't indulge the 'how-can-he-do-this-to-me' attitude?" I nodded and said, "That's exactly what I am saying."

We then discussed how a more humble attitude would prompt her to accept that Martin is the way he is and realize that she should not expect favored treatment from him. It simply was not meant to be. She could likewise stop trying to reform him with pleading arguments and could drop her shocked response that he didn't act more respect-fully toward her. He was not going to reform, and no matter how dis-tasteful his behavior was, she would need to factor his arrogance into every interaction. She did not have to like him or agree with his ways, but she could accept the reality that he did not care about her feelings and that he would not consider her needs in future decisions. She would let go of any illusion that he would hold her in high regard.

Cindy and I discussed how humility would actually strengthen her responses to Martin. Instead of following her wishful feelings, she would use reason and reality to guide her. Pride caused her to obsess on the question, "Why won't he treat me well?" Humility will allow her to anchor in the thought, "When he doesn't treat me well, I can move on without his blessing. I don't require favored treatment from him because he is not God. His proclamations are not the ultimate." Her humility would spare her the fruitless desire to be esteemed by one who had no intention or ability to esteem her.

Humble people accept that life sometimes is painful. Though they do not relish pain, neither do they fall apart when it appears. They enjoy being treated well, yet they do not demand that others act correctly before they can proceed with confidence. Humble peo-ple can be assertive, yet their assertions do not carry the require-ment that the other person must like them or agree with them. They have rightly concluded that trials, while uncomfortable, do not define who they are or how they will conduct themselves.

### Living with Humility

Humility involves both a shift in thinking and acting. As you choose to give less priority to your prideful impulses and opt instead to respond to narcissism with humility, you will notice that your healthy responses will come to the fore. Your humility will be evidence of your spiritual well-being. In the following sections I outline the steps to accomplish that goal.

**1. Be Respectful, Even When Respect Is Not Reciprocated.** As we've seen, an identifying feature of narcissism is a feeling of entitlement. Narcissists crave respect, to the extent that they are convinced that others are grossly mistaken when they do not give them the highest regard. So strong is the narcissistic need to be admired that they can respond with great anger or rejection when it is not fully given. Even the slightest evidence of disregard can bring out a narcissist's wrath, and the resulting demand for respect is not likely to be conveyed respectfully. This makes it easy for you, the recipient of the disrespectful communication, to respond in the same manner.

Randall was a man who had to be ultracautious whenever his brother-in-law, Cliff, visited for the holidays. Cliff could initially be friendly and gregarious, but Randall had learned to treat Cliff with special deference if he wanted to avoid Cliff's scorn. For instance, Randall liked to joke with his nieces and nephews at family gatherings, but early in their relationship he realized that his brother-in-law could not tolerate any kidding. He was likely to interpret it as an insult, and it could easily send him into pouting and withdrawal. Cliff had very precise notions about the way he should be treated, and he would tolerate no deviance from his exacting (and pride-filled) standards. Over time, Randall learned that Cliff said disparaging things about him to mutual acquaintances. And that offended him. Randall explained to me that he wanted to speak frankly about this problem with Cliff, yet he knew Cliff was too self-absorbed to discuss the problem maturely. As the years had passed, Randall learned to distrust his brother-in-law's gestures of friendliness, and now he wondered if he should confront him about this talking behind Randall's back.

Whereas Randall could have justified an agitated and angry response to Cliff, I advised him not to respond to his brother-in-law's prideful spirit with his own bruised pride. If Cliff behaved as a thin-skinned person or spoke poorly about him to others, that did not need to send Randall into a fit of insecurity. Instead, Randall could humbly remind himself that some family relationships are less than ideal, and he did not have to have perfect circumstances in order to behave respectfully. While he might never feel close to Cliff, he did not have to lose sleep over the prospect of having a shallow relationship with his brother-in-law.

Many of us make the mistake of assuming that respect must be earned before it is given. While you might not respect a narcissist, you can still treat that person with respect. Notice in the following illustrations how this might work:

- A narcissist speaks with great sarcasm and condescension toward you, yet you determine that your demeanor will remain dignified.

- The narcissist cannot engage in a conversation without repeatedly turning the attention back toward herself. You can maintain a patient spirit rather than displaying open annoyance.

- The narcissist might pitch a raging fit, screaming and cursing. You can refrain from shouting your response as you recognize that it is fruitless to become drawn into an angry battle of wills.

Humble individuals recognize that they cannot cause life to unfold ideally. While they certainly prefer that others treat them well, they do not demand that all go according to plan before they can be civil. Narcissists, in the spirit of pride, must first have their way, then they *might* decide to show respect. Their pleasant behavior, however, can be interpreted as manipulation since it is linked to the way others treat them. In contrast, humble people are dignified, not because they believe their behavior can be an effective tool to control others, but because they have made dignity a part of their character.

**2. Refrain from Power Communications.** Narcissists live with the delusion that others will conform to their standards once they have a proper understanding of the facts (in other words, once they agree that the narcissist is indeed superior). When narcissists encounter others who will not succumb to their logic or preferences, they predictably try force. They can become stubborn and aggressive, and they honestly believe it is their duty to make others conform to their preferences.

In Chapter Four we saw how Barbara struggled to gain assistance from her passive-aggressive brother, Donald, as she tended to the needs of their elderly father. He was unreliable on the occasions when he promised to help, and he was evasive when she attempted to pin him down with specific commitments. Once, after Donald had reneged on a promise to help their dad with some needed household repairs, she confronted him angrily about his latest episode of selfishness. "What is *wrong* with you?" she blurted out. "Every time I try to get you to show a little regard for Dad, you fumble the ball. You are the most pigheaded person on the planet, and I'm tired of having to cover for your incompetence."

Donald's face turned beet red as he replied, "You have no business trying to tell me how to prioritize my life! I'll do as I dang well please, and if you don't like it, you can take your prissy attitude and shove it where the sun don't shine." As you might imagine, a heated argument ensued, and ugly accusations flew both ways. Donald was not a man of many words, but once he opened the verbal floodgates, there was no holding back. The argument was loud and long, leaving each emotionally depleted. They vowed never to speak with the other again.

As I later spoke with Barbara, she huffed as she told me, "That man thinks of no one beyond himself. It's like he lives in a world where no one besides him has needs. Whenever I try to talk with him about helping out, he'll either invalidate what I'm saying or go into an attack mode. Either way, I can't get through to him." When I asked how she tended to respond when he became argumentative, she replied, "It usually doesn't get me anywhere, but I argue right back with him. I can get pretty riled up."

Barbara's frustration was certainly legitimate, yet she made the mistake of responding to her brother with a spirit of pride that tried to force him to do what she felt he should do. In his egotistical approach to family responsibilities, Donald operated with the notion that his preferences were to be given highest priority, and if others didn't like it, that was too bad. In her angry responses to him, Barbara often displayed an "I'll-show-you-who's-boss" mentality, which only made matters worse. Her prideful attitudes were not as extreme as her brother's, yet her forcefulness implied that she was thinking, "You have no right to do anything counter to what I say. I will *force* you to cooperate!"

Sitting in my office, when Barbara examined her exchanges with her brother objectively, she openly admitted that she often responded to his selfish behavior with her own version of selfish anger. She paused momentarily then asked, "But what other options do I have? I've got to make him listen!"

I mentioned that before we spelled out some communication adjustments, first she would need to reconsider the thinking that preceded her words. She mistakenly assumed that Donald owed it to her to adjust when she gave him directives. Her pride prompted her to assume that he was obligated to her, which he was not. In humility, she would need to remember that the world did not revolve around her, and despite the inappropriateness of his behaviors, he was a grown man who had the prerogative to think for himself. Barbara looked at me quizzically and said, "Am I supposed to just go along with his sorry attitude even when he is clearly in the wrong? Is that what you are telling me?" I responded that she would need to drop the insinuation that there was a clear way her brother *must* respond. She would need to recognize that once she spoke her opinions, he was free to respond as he pleased, even if his response was ill advised. She could begin by humbly accepting her limitations in her relationship with Donald.

If you can embrace humility in the midst of your conflicts with a narcissist, you can adopt a different style of communication. Rather than responding to power with power, you can respond with calm

COMMITTING TO HUMILITY 151

firmness. Rather than being insistent or persuasive, you can remain true to your convictions even as you allow the other person to choose freely his or her response, no matter how misguided it might be. Rather than speaking stubbornly in response to the narcissist's stubbornness, you can resist the temptation to force your will as you establish reasonable boundaries.

As I encourage individuals such as Barbara to stay out of power plays, I sometimes hear the protest, "But if I maintain humility, the other person will just go his merry way and make no changes." I usually agree with this conclusion, then I remind them that the goal of any communication with a narcissist is not to overpower that person's reasoning but to remain true to your own convictions. Humble people recognize that they cannot force others to fit a mold, and they make no attempt to bring them into submission. Retaining emotional stability, even when the other person is clearly unstable, is the primary goal.

**3. Accept That the Narcissist Might Think Ill of You.** None of us likes knowing that another holds a low opinion of us. People such as Cindy, Randall, and Barbara could recount many occasions when the narcissist openly indicated or subtly insinuated that they thought they were stupid. Insulting attitudes are common when you are in conflict with a narcissist, and the narcissist will frequently ridicule ideas and preferences that seem perfectly normal to you.

Cindy, in particular, struggled knowing that Martin had a chronically low regard for her character. Throughout their marriage he had belittled her and had unabashedly communicated that he believed she was a dolt whose opinions were useless. I could not fault her for protesting such foul treatment, yet I wanted her to recognize that she could maintain self-esteem not by reforming him but by taming the pride that kept her tied to his wrong opinions.

Frequently when Martin had displayed low regard for her, she would think something like, "I can't believe he treats me this way." I gently confronted her by asking, "Why in the world would you have a hard time believing that he looks down on you? He's been doing it for years, and it's not just you that he disdains, it's virtually anyone who does not think like him." I was asking her to abandon her emotions about those interactions and instead look logically at the way Martin's mind works. Cindy sat upright and then smiled sheepishly as she said, "I guess you have a good point. It should be no surprise that he would insult me one more time, given the fact that he's done it hundreds of times before." I challenged her to admit that, barring a miracle, ten years from now he would still think she was an idiot. Nothing short of her agreeing with his every decision would convince him that she had a good brain. She needed to drop the delusion that it would be otherwise.

In pride we can assume that others are obligated to think well of us, giving compliments instead of complaints and accepting us in the midst of our humanness. That represents a noble ideal, but it does not match reality. Pride tends to keep us trapped in best-case thinking and causes us to wish desperately that we could somehow be immune from the hurts that are so common in a flawed world. Though we may not use these exact words, pride can get us thinking, "I should be the first person in history who won't have to suffer the humiliation of knowing that significant others have a low opinion of me."

In humility we know that insults exist, and no one is exempt from them, no matter what. A humble person will not feel comfortable embracing the reality of rejection and degradation yet will experience no shock when those unpleasant things happen. For instance, Cindy recognized that Martin's arrogance would not allow him to admit that his selfishness had caused many of their past conflicts; instead he'd continue to believe that she must be to blame. As twisted as his logic was, his reasoning made sense to him. In her humility, Cindy could accept that no pleading from her would cause him to elevate his opinion of her. Likewise, Barbara would need to accept that her brother, Donald, honestly believed that his evasive approach to life was reasonable, and furthermore, he could fully rationalize that her chosen way of life was deficient. Similarly, Randall would need to accept that as Cliff sulked and pouted in the

aftermath of their exchanges, Cliff truly believed he was right to reject Randall.

A defining feature of narcissism is the inability to incorporate
others' reality. When we witness how readily they criticize and belittle, our pride can prompt us to think that they shouldn't think
that way, that they should think the way we do. In doing so, we
mimic the narcissist's pride. Humble people know they cannot get
inside a narcissist's mind, rearranging their core thoughts and beliefs. Even when they are the object of derision and scorn, they accept that some people have very limited capacities to love, and the
result of such limitation could be that they will be poorly esteemed.

**4. *Release Your Disillusionment and Move On.*** Repeated
episodes of distressing experiences with a narcissist can leave you
feeling weary and disillusioned. As narcissists show their incapabil-
ity of love and acceptance, it is only natural that you regret that the
relationship has fallen short of its potential. In most cases, the relationship with the narcissist began with the promise of a rewarding
exchange typified by good-natured conversation and encouragement. Time, however, has shown that not only does the narcissist
refuse to change, but negative traits greatly outweigh the positive.
The feeling of futility is a common byproduct.

Sometimes this futility takes the form of depression, while at
other times it leaves the recipient of foul treatment feeling tense
and edgy. Barbara, for instance, told me that when she knew she
would encounter her brother at family events, she began anticipating upset feelings. Even when he acted pleasantly, she maintained
the bitter belief that it was only a matter of time until he would say
or do something distasteful. She explained, "I guess my hurt feelings
are made worse by the fact that I would never treat family members
the way he does. I have witnessed him being pleasant with people
in public, and that makes me wonder why he is so uncaring with
those he should be most loyal toward."

I could not argue with Barbara's logic, but everything she had
told me about her brother led me to believe that she could wait

years without experiencing consistent cooperation from Donald. She could not afford to let her feelings hinge on his behaviors and attitudes. She needed to lay down the hope that he would be any different, and she could only do so by humbly accepting that her brother would probably never learn to see life from her perspective. By accepting him as he was, she could release him from the requirement to be the kind of brother she wanted, and more important, she could free herself to be the best she could be in the rest of her relationships.

Barbara once mentioned to me that it did not seem right to accept Donald, knowing as she did that he would continue his uncaring attitudes. I told Barbara that, at this point, I was not so worried about Donald's next move. Unfortunately, he didn't seem concerned enough to make the needed adjustments. I was more concerned that Barbara's ongoing disillusionment could cause her to become so preoccupied with the effects of his foul treatment that it would rob her of the good traits in her personality. It would be very unfortunate if she were swallowed up by gloom and cynicism.

Humble individuals hold strong beliefs about right and wrong, yet those beliefs are not so powerful as to trap them in self-absorbed feelings that ruin their ability to interact successfully with others. They understand that they have many good traits to offer other people, so they refuse to allow narcissists to keep them from utilizing those traits. Without arrogance, they conclude that they must stay on mission to share the best parts of themselves with those who can appreciate what they have to offer. By moving away from the narcissist, they indeed concede defeat, yet they also show that they refuse to allow the narcissist to remain in control of their deliberations.

## Refusing to Play God

The self-absorption of narcissists can sometimes seem so extreme that it illustrates that they have elevated themselves to godlike status. No one can tell narcissists what is right because in their own godlike way they have already determined what is right and wrong. So shallow is their willingness to accept others' input that they can hardly ever make concessions. As you determine the best way to respond to such an attitude, you will be tempted to argue your case strongly. Don't allow this to happen, though, and remind yourself that you are highly unlikely to redirect the mind of a god.

Your commitment to humility will likewise illustrate that you have no interest in imitating a deity. As you accept your limited capacity to orchestrate life according to your mandates, you will experience a freedom that the narcissist will never know. Cindy once used an analogy as she explained how she was coming to terms with Martin's unwillingness to change his selfish ways. "I try to picture what a factory worker's job is like. He has his place on the assembly line and is expected to take care of the task directly in front of him. He's not up in the boardroom making the decisions affecting all the other workers; he's a specialist who understands that he can only do so much to keep the project running smoothly. I'm realizing how I've wished I could be the one in the boardroom as it relates to my relationship with Martin. For so long I've wondered how I could manage him as he interacts with me and our kids, but like the line worker, I can determine instead to take care of what is in front of me and not worry about making him do his job correctly." Cindy correctly surmised that Martin's life was driven by a defiance of all authority, so it would be folly to assume that he would submit to hers.

To maintain a humble spirit, you will need to possess a sufficient amount of inner confidence. We will explore that topic in Chapter Nine.

*Chapter Nine*

# Fostering Your Own Inner Security

Sandi came to me because she had discovered that Justin, her husband of twelve years, had had two affairs, was a frequent user of pornography, and had admitted that he often went to strip clubs. He had been deceiving Sandi about all of this throughout their entire marriage. From the beginning Justin had been edgy and temperamental, so they had never developed the communication skills that would have helped them resolve their differences. To make matters worse, Justin was very reluctant to confront the seriousness of his misdeeds, choosing instead to blame Sandi for their problems.

As I talked further with Sandi, it became clear that she had struggled with insecurity most of her life. Born into a family dominated by an angry, controlling father, she had learned early in life to act in carefully calculated ways. Though she was an intelligent person, she had never learned to trust her own decisions. The constant criticism from her father and husband had caused her to become quite anxious and uncertain when she faced even common decisions.

"I learned by accident that Justin was going to the strip clubs," she told me, "and I learned about his infidelity only because one of my girlfriends had been told about it by her husband. Justin would never have admitted it if my friend had not discovered it first." She began crying as she said, "Justin is making me out to be the one who has all the problems. He told me that none of this would have happened if I had been the wife he needed. He accused me of not being good in bed. He said that I pay too much attention to our daughter and that is why he felt lonely and isolated. He accused me of being

157

too defensive, saying that is why we don't have good communication. To hear him explain it, you would think he is a perfect angel who just had the bad fortune of being married to some wicked witch."

As I listened to Sandi describe her circumstances, it became increasingly clear that Justin had all the core ingredients of a narcissist: a controlling nature, a sense of entitlement, exploitive behavior, an unwillingness to receive unflattering input, and a poor comprehension of reality. Indeed, Justin illustrated the extent of his narcissistic leanings when he insisted that Sandi, not he, was the one who needed counseling. Naturally, Sandi was angry and fearful; the prospect of divorce loomed large, and she did not relish the possibility of having to struggle as a single mom. As I got to know Sandi, I saw that she needed help with her tendency to accept shame and guilt. So accustomed was she to receiving Justin's accusations as true that she had lost much of her ability to deal with them. She had entered adulthood with a shaky foundation for self-esteem due to her father's oppressive nature, and now she had the additional burden of knowing that her husband too held her in low regard. This was proving to be more than she felt she could manage. As a primary thrust of my work with her, we sought to address how she could build an inner foundation of confidence that would allow her to maintain her own security.

## Imbalances in Dependency

In very different ways, both Justin and Sandi's behavior indicated that they each had an *imbalanced dependency*; that is, they both relied on external factors to influence their inner mood or sense of direction. Though Justin was too proud to admit it, he had spent much of his life desperately looking for people to affirm him, a phenomenon that is common among narcissists. Charming and fun-loving, Justin wanted others to find him attractive and desirable. He had to drive the right kind of vehicle, dress in the latest fashion, be connected with "in" people, and be known for his successes. His inclinations toward sexually exploitive behavior could be interpreted as a craving to be connected with women in a manner that fed his ego, because he needed their affirmation to compensate for his hidden insecurity.

Sandi, on the other hand, displayed her dependency by allowing her husband to play too much of a role in determining her sense of worth. Not as gregarious and socially adept as Justin, she often wondered if others found her appealing and fretted about the ways others might interpret her flaws or her unique preferences. For instance, often after a social event, Justin would recount ways she had not handled herself correctly (in other words, the way he wanted her to act). Instead of confidently maintaining the belief that she had been perfectly appropriate in her interactions, she worried that she had indeed embarrassed herself and Justin. The pattern continued in many other ways; Sandi gave Justin too much power to determine her moods and her sense of herself.

It is not wrong or unusual for one's moods to be tied to others' words or actions. We each have yearnings to be affirmed and connected to others, so it is natural to want to be accepted. Being dependent is not a problem unless it is carried to extremes. When we experience chronic anxiety, discouragement, anger, and the like, it is a sign that our dependencies have gotten out of control, that we are putting our emotional stability into the hands of people who do not have our best interests at heart.

If all this sounds familiar to you, consider the following expressions of imbalanced dependencies:

- Others' opinions strongly influence your decisions, particularly if they are likely to question your decision.
- When another person is angry, you feel stuck in unwanted frustration.
- You work too hard to plead your case when another person disagrees with you.
- Another person's foul mood can put you into a foul mood.

- Though you intend to be consistently respectful, those good intentions are sidetracked when others prove to be difficult.
- When criticized, you quickly become defensive.
- When others maltreat you, you fume as you ask yourself, "Why do I have to put up with this nonsense?"
- You soothe your frustrations through overeating, drinking, shopping, or some other diversionary tactic.
- You attempt to appease others as a means of avoiding conflict.
- The way you present yourself on the outside is not always consistent with what you feel on the inside.
- Feelings of hurt linger a long time.

The key to understanding imbalanced dependency is to recognize when you give too much power to others over how you conduct your life. You might not be consciously aware of the extent to which you allow others to affect you, but you can become more aware as you learn to recognize the signals of exaggerated dependency on the narcissists in your life.

## Nurturing Your Own Competence and Independence

Ideally, all of us would reach adulthood years with tried-and-true ways of handling conflict, but most adults do not have a history of being challenged to know how to manage their feelings during times of intense pressure. Their emotional stability hinges precariously on what others do. Instead of learning to be competent in emotional management skills, they remain emotionally dependent and incompetent, unwittingly conceding their emotional well-being to others. When that other person is a narcissist, this becomes a formula for disaster. Narcissists cannot be satisfied until you do what they expect. If you make different decisions or have other preferences, narcissists are likely to make it clear that you are obligated to conform to their standards, and if you do not, you will surely suffer the consequences of their anger, which will be met in turn by your own anger, uncertainty, guilt, futility, disillusionment, and be-wilderment. To avoid this nasty syndrome, you need a well-defined course of action that will guide you and keep you from letting their moods and preferences determine your own.

As I spoke with Sandi about her persistently conflicted emotions, she admitted that Justin's moods or declarations affected her in-tensely. When he criticized, she second-guessed. When he shouted, she defended unnecessarily. When he blamed, she accepted guilt she didn't deserve. When he withdrew, she assumed it was her fault. As we talked, we acknowledged that she had an imbalance in her dependencies, but there was another insight I wanted her to incor-porate. I said, "Sandi, when you fall into these troubled responses each time Justin mistreats you, it seems as though you have given up on being able to recognize and maintain your own more stable feelings—regardless of what he does or says. You're giving him a lot of power that is not really his to hold."

She nodded as she replied, "You're not the first person to point this out. I know I let him have too much power over my moods, but I can't seem to help myself."

"That sentiment needs to go," I said quickly. "While it is re-grettable that Justin does not treat you the way you'd like, you are not helpless. Over the years you might have bought into the notion that you can't get it together, but that simply is not true. You have more competence and more security within you than you realize."

I pointed out to Sandi that she overused the word *can't* as she considered how she should respond to Justin's selfish behaviors. The word surfaced in statements such as the following:

- "I can't deal with this anymore."
- "I can't stop feeling so discouraged."
- "There is no way I can get him to understand me. I can't ever say the right things."
- "I can't muster any optimism as long as he mistreats me."

As we continued talking, I explained, "Sure enough, there are some things outside your control. You can't make Justin be considerate or

act less rudely or be more flexible. But you can choose different responses when he is difficult. You are not without options." We went
on to discuss and practice ways for her to calmly hold her ground
when they disagreed, to stop defending herself unnecessarily and
follow through on her own decisions even when he was being bossy.
I wanted her to remember that she had a good mind and that it was
reasonable to follow her own instincts.

"The deeper problem I'm wanting you to see," I explained, "is
your tendency to assume that you are doomed to miserable emotions once it becomes clear that you and Justin disagree."

As Sandi and I talked about how easily she acquiesced to Justin's
moods, we tied this trend to a pattern that had been established during her developmental years. Very early in life she had learned that
it was not good to have thoughts or feelings that differed from her father's. Being forceful and stubborn, he frequently belittled her when
she expressed separate needs or viewpoints. She recalled, "I remember determining that I'd better not be too open about my preferences
until I first filtered things through my dad. If there were a chance
that he would get mad or put me down, I'd hold my tongue. The
older I got, the more risky it seemed to be unique."

"It sounds to me like you were not given the chance to develop
confidence in your decision-making processes," I observed. She nodded, which then prompted me to ask a follow-up question, "When
your dad shut you down, does that mean that you stopped being
competent?"

"I guess not, now that you put it that way," she replied. "I never
really thought much about my general competence, at least as it is
related to emotions. Are you trying to lead me toward the conclusion that I have more positive skills within myself than I have learned
to use?"

I nodded as I said, "That's exactly right."

Narcissists would like you to believe that you are incompetent,
because that makes it easier for them to control you. You'll always
think they're right, and life continues to conveniently revolve
around them. For instance, Sandi's dad would have done well by

her if he had chosen during her early years to talk with her about ways to handle childhood hurts and frustrations as opposed to being so concerned with controlling her every move. Because of his narcissism, however, he was so focused on himself that he hardly ever thought about his role in caring for Sandi's emotional well-being. Likewise, Justin would have been a more suitable husband if he had chosen to work with Sandi to coordinate their lives and foster each other's satisfaction. He could have indicated that he found Sandi an equal partner and that he valued her input into their decisions. But he too was too self-absorbed to look beyond his own cravings, which led him to dismiss Sandi as if she were a person of little consequence.

Chronic exposure to these devaluing messages can leave people such as Sandi feeling as if they have little power over their own lives. Faced with the narcissist's anger or dominance, they assume that it is impossible to move forward with any hope. These people make the mistake of assuming that their quality of life depends so heavily on the narcissist that they forget that they can find peace and strength without the narcissist's blessing.

### Intervene on Your Own Behalf

Narcissists like nothing more than to squelch their partner's thinking and ability to make separate decisions, but that doesn't mean that you have to acquiesce. For instance, Justin would micromanage Sandi whenever they were out in public. He would criticize her table manners, her posture, her conversation with friends, and her clothing. Over the years, she had come to anticipate these criticisms and had gotten in the habit of allowing anxiety to rule as she worried about upsetting him. This did not have to be.

I explained to her, "Sandi, it seems as if you have handed your brain to Justin and that you have given him permission to program it as he will. That's nuts!"

She smiled sheepishly as she replied, "Okay, I'll admit that it doesn't make sense to let him be so influential, so what are you suggesting?"

"I'm suggesting that you give yourself permission to draw upon your deepest beliefs as they pertain to each situation in which you and Justin differ. Act upon your own good judgment even if he doesn't agree."

Before a person such as Sandi can be as decisive as necessary, she needs to take time to contemplate the deeper questions about life. Who am I? What is my mission? What unique strengths do I have, and how can they best be used? When is it good to be cooperative, and when is it necessary to be going my own way? Why did God create me to be different from all other people, and what implications does that have as I interact with others? What does it mean to be responsible, to myself and to others? These questions and many others do not have to be filtered through the narcissist. They can be answered on their own, in accord with each person's gifts and life purpose. Not to ponder such matters is irresponsible.

Since narcissists are not emotionally mature enough to accommodate others' independent thinking, it is predictable that they will resist your efforts to think for yourself. They will tell you you're wrong or stupid or ill advised. Keep in mind that this person has only his or her interests at heart—not yours. Don't make the mistake of being derailed by their derision, and don't make it your job to appease them. You cannot gain a narcissist's approval, so you need to give up on getting it. Sandi began realizing that Justin's inability to accept her as an equal was so entrenched that she needed to stop hoping that she could somehow gain his approval. She was a bright woman with reasonable ideas about life, and if Justin could not see that, it was not her problem to solve. She needed to give herself permission to do as she deemed appropriate with or without his cooperation. Because she was such a kindhearted woman, such a notion initially seemed harsh to her, but upon further reflection she recognized that she was remaining in unhealthy relationship patterns as long as she allowed him to set her pace. The emotional despair she was experiencing when she came to see me was a signal that she could no longer afford to remain in the dysfunctional patterns of her relationship with Justin.

## Use Right Thinking to Break the Cycle

As you separate yourself from another's narcissistic manipulations, you will be poised to chart your own course as opposed to letting the narcissist do it for you. Let's examine some key ideas that can guide you in this effort.

*1. You Can Commit to Your God-Given Worth.* As narcissists attempt to gain the upper hand in relationships, they refuse to acknowledge a core truth about humanity: each person has innate worth that exists from the day of birth and continues throughout life. For instance, you can probably recall many scenes when you expressed a preference or opinion only to have the narcissist dismiss your thinking as unacceptable. Or perhaps the narcissist ridiculed your feelings or labeled your perceptions as wrong or interrupted you to correct you or inject a better idea. Such incidents reflect the narcissist's inability to accept that others have just as much value as they do.

Rather than collapsing under their condescension or working to prove them wrong, you can work toward becoming inwardly anchored in your inherent worth. Consider the fundamentals that are instinctively communicated at the very beginning of life. On your day of birth, what did the attendants do when you first entered the world? Did they yawn and set you off to the side, only to return a few hours later to see what you were doing? Of course not! They gave you full priority and tended to your every need. You were the center of attention, treated with the utmost care. Why did this happen? Those present at your birth knew instinctively that you had great worth simply because you existed, period. Your inclusion in the human family makes you valuable even before you can perform or appease. Human worth is not a commodity that some have and some do not. It is an integral part of each person's identity and is not subject to the arbitrary pronouncements of self-appointed judges. Even if key people—mothers, fathers, siblings, teachers, spouses, friends, and acquaintances—do a poor job of acknowledging your intrinsic worth, it never ceases to exist. Misguided humans cannot overrule human worth and dignity. When some people choose to treat others as though they had little worth, it only indicates their weak grasp of a very fundamental tenet.

Justin was so wrapped up in his own self-importance that he had become incapable of treating his wife as one who was worthy. Ideally he would have reinforced her worth by listening to her feelings and reflections, by consistently paying her sincere compliments, by being flexible in lifestyle decisions, and by considering her needs when he set his own priorities. The fact that he rarely did these things did not mean that Sandi had no worth but that he was deficient in some very fundamental life skills.

As Sandi progressed in counseling, she realized that Justin's poor treatment of her was a commentary about his own troubled psyche, not hers. She began looking for ways to underscore her belief in her core worth even as it remained clear that Justin would not. For instance, she stopped accepting his proclamations as irrefutably true and began to act upon her separate convictions. Additionally, she stopped seeking him out for approval when making simple financial or domestic decisions and chose instead to follow her common sense. Likewise, she stopped responding to his insults with crying or anger. Instead, she disciplined herself to sift through his words objectively; if they were untrue, she would continue without the need to make him reform or recant his erroneous statements.

"I feel so relieved," she told me, "to recognize that I do not have to concede to him the godlike power he wants to have over me. I think it is only fair that I treat him with dignity, since he is a human who deserves fairness just as anyone else would. When he cannot reciprocate that same treatment, it's not a reflection of my value." As she spoke these words, I knew that she was catching on to the idea that she no longer had to be emotionally dependent on him to feel good herself.

**2. You Can Commit to Honesty.** When people such as Sandi allow their moods to depend upon narcissists such as Justin, an unsettling pattern begins to develop. Wanting peace or relief at any cost, they can become less than honest as they attempt to say or do whatever it takes to get out of the narcissist's hold. Though the majority of people contending with narcissists are not chronic liars, neither do they feel safe enough to be truly open about who they are and what they believe. The narcissist can be so overpowering that it's safer to hide differing opinions. That can lead to having to maintain a false front.

Before Sandi sought counseling, she had developed a habit of not revealing her activities to Justin or not saying what she believed and felt. "It had become so stressful for me to show him that I had different preferences that I became convinced I should do whatever was expedient to keep him off my back. If I had spent a few more dollars than he would have wanted me to spend, I'd sidestep his questions when he asked me about expenses. Or if I had allowed our daughter to do something I knew he would gripe about, we just wouldn't talk about it. I had become very calculated, even sneaky, about what I would reveal because I had learned that I'd better filter every decision through the grid of his volatile emotions."

Dishonesty is not part of a healthy lifestyle. Emotionally independent people determine for themselves how they will live, and they do not allow others to set their agenda for them. When they encounter narcissists who seem to require dishonesty or sneaking around, they can choose healthiness over compliance even if it creates strains in the relationship. For instance, once Sandi spent a summer afternoon with her daughter watching a movie. She debated whether she should even tell her husband about their outing, and in the past she would not have brought up the subject. Recognizing, however, that her calculated thinking was causing her to feel deceptive, she determined that she and her daughter would speak openly about the day's activities. If he expressed disapproval, she would accept it and not try to appease him.

Emotionally dependent people do not feel that they can approach life straightforwardly. They are easy targets for narcissistic manipulations, because they worry too much about the ways the narcissist will respond. They mistakenly take on the responsibility of keeping the other person happy even when it forces them to be phony. The result is emotional confusion, because they can never feel certain that they are doing what will appease the narcissist. Developing honesty about their true beliefs and priorities can seem risky, but compared to the alternative of deception and dishonesty, the benefits greatly outweigh the risks.

**3. You Can Use Truth as an Emotional Shock Absorber.** Often people who are dependent upon a narcissist are shocked when they encounter rude or rejecting behaviors. For instance, if you have made a decision that a narcissist dislikes, you are likely to get some sort of negative treatment such as criticism, silent withdrawal, or bossiness. How do you tend to respond to such treatment? Dependent individuals usually recoil, thinking, "I can't believe I have to endure this," or "This can't really be happening to me." Their minds reel with disbelief that they are on the receiving end of the narcissist's gross insensitivity. Even those who have had hundreds of poor responses from a narcissist are still shocked at the next instance. The reason for this is that dependent individuals have such strong hopes that others will be what they need that they stubbornly cling to the false notion that the other person will give responses they want or need. Such thinking is counterproductive. The truth is that they cannot rely on others, particularly narcissists, to give them what they expect.

As Sandi recounted her history of tension with her husband, she admitted that it was difficult to accept that he could be so consistently unloving and inflexible. She reflected out loud, "As a girl, I always held out the hope that my daddy would become proud of me and treat me the ways I saw my friends' dads treat them. Every now and then he would say something nice or show favoritism toward me, but it was rare. Whenever he would ignore me or gripe and yell, inwardly I would wonder what I was supposed to do to make him act nice. I naively assumed that if I could learn the right ways to approach him, things would change for the better. Of course, they never did.

"When I married Justin, I had really believed that I had found the person who would be proud of me and would treat me with the kindness and respect I wanted. When we dated, he treated me like a lady, but once we married it seemed like a switch flipped in his brain rendering him incapable of being consistently nice. I became so disillusioned, and maybe that is something I've not fully recovered from."

Sandi's desires for love from both her father and husband were reasonable, yet they did not match reality. Though it is disillusioning to admit the truth, neither man seemed to possess the desire or willpower to curb his selfish behaviors long enough to factor in her needs. In retrospect she was able to recognize that even their nice behaviors were manipulative attempts to get what they wanted.

It can be difficult to accept the ugly truth that some individuals are so completely self-absorbed that they cannot sustain love. Nonetheless, in the case of narcissism, that is reality. You can work overtime trying to change it, but it will remain what it is.

Rather than registering shock that a narcissist will be selfish or insensitive, you can choose to accept the truth, no matter how disappointing it might be. In Sandi's case, she had to admit that Justin was not the white knight she had once assumed he would be. Practically, this meant that she would refrain from pleading with him to give her the loving treatment she wanted but that he could not give. She would let go of her insistent tone of voice when she talked with him about her separate preferences. She would rely less on him for words of encouragement and draw more from friends and from her spiritual beliefs. Making these adjustments generated feelings of grief and sadness, since it meant letting go of a dream, yet it also freed her to look elsewhere for personal peace.

It is easy to accept truth that happens to coincide with what we want, but a mark of a balanced person is the willingness to accept truth that runs counter to our personal desires. It illustrates that we have stopped looking to others to provide stability but have committed to staying focused on our own personal mission.

**4. *You Can Set Aside Black-and-White Thinking.*** Black-and-white thinkers like it when life (and people) operate in fixed, predictable ways. They have convinced themselves that they cannot live with the flaws and disappointments that are an inevitable part of relationships. They can be very dogmatic in their beliefs about right and wrong, and they expend much energy trying to make the narcissists in their lives agree with them despite much evidence that this will never happen. Though the narcissist will be predictably uncooperative or argumentative, dependent individuals still press their fixed ideas of how life should unfold and are unwilling to accept the reality that the narcissist cannot appreciate their seemingly airtight reasoning.

In one of my early sessions with Sandi I asked her to recall how often she and Justin clashed on common lifestyle matters. I detected from our conversations that this was a pervasive problem, and she confirmed that they argued often about the same old problems. "You have developed very strong principles about correct living, but that is something Justin will never appreciate. I know it seems odd to suggest that you can be right too often, but in your case, your sense of correctness actually keeps you from being healthy emotionally, because you are working too hard to convince him of your beliefs. Each time he disagrees, you take it as an invitation to go to battle, and that is not good. You'll need to stop insisting that he adhere to your fixed agenda and concentrate instead on seeing the situation more realistically."

"So I'm just supposed to give up my convictions? Is that what you're trying to tell me? I can't do that because it would feel as if I'm being untrue to myself." Frustration was written all over Sandi's face as she pondered the possibility of letting Justin have his way.

I explained, "I'm not suggesting that you drop your beliefs. Not at all. I am suggesting that you spend less time trying to reform

Justin and more time tending to your own emotional stability. This means you accept that there is going to be a lot of gray in your life. Try as hard as you want, but you're not going to coerce Justin into living in a manner that will bring you peace."

To further clarify this point, I explained to Sandi, "I'm not saying that it is never a good idea to confront a narcissist. Sometimes you need to establish self-respect by standing up for your convictions. I *am* saying, though, that it will be rare for a narcissist to digest your words carefully and make the adjustments you want. Rather than wasting your emotional energy trying to reform a mule-headed person, you'll need to focus instead on how you will proceed without his agreement or cooperation. This means that you will need to release him from the requirement to be your all-in-all."

When you insist that others meet your black-and-white criteria before you can move forward, you are quietly giving yourself an insult. It is as if you are saying, "I'll fall apart if I don't get his cooperation." That does not have to be. You have the strength to adjust to difficult circumstances, even when they do not meet your strict standards.

I explained to Sandi, "There is definitely a degree of pessimism that accompanies my approach with narcissistic individuals. While it feels wonderful to dream that you could speak the right words that would generate the ideal response, it simply is not going to happen. When you cling desperately to the belief that the narcissist will reform, you only invite pain. You'll need to settle into the realization that life with Justin will never meet your perfect standards."

In Sandi's case, she spent the next months rearranging the ways she conducted her life so Justin would not be such a dominant influence in her decisions. She learned to trust more in her parental decisions. She chose social activities based on her criteria and priorities, not his. She defended less and remained firm when her schedule conflicted with his commands. Often Justin voiced his displeasure loudly, but instead of cowering or pleading her case, she told him that she heard his perspective, yet she also continued to believe that it was right to follow her own reasoning.

You too can separate your moods and directions from the narcissist in your life. As you examine your history with that person, you will likely recall few moments when he or she truly looked out for your best interests. This can prompt you to adjust your responses so that you rely less on his or her participation in your life, drawing instead on your own beliefs. Such an adjustment will probably run counter to your fixed notions regarding the good life, yet it will result in you being more consistent with your life's mission, not the narcissist's twisted mission.

## Chapter Ten

# Replacing Bitterness
# with Forgiveness

Shannon was a forty-year-old mother of three who felt at the end of her rope in her relationship with her parents. "My father is the most pushy person I know," she told me. "He owns his company, which means that he gets to tell his employees what to do without worrying about accountability. If he doesn't like the way an employee responds, he fires that person right there on the spot. He handles family members in much the same way, although he can't fire us," she said with a wry smile. "He's the boss, period. If one of his children dislikes his decisions, he will stubbornly determine how to proceed and won't take any input from anyone. If we don't like his rulings, too bad. Dad bends to no one."

She went on. "My mother has had a love-hate relationship with Dad for as long as I can remember. She argues with him vehemently over minor matters, but when I express similar frustrations with Dad, she shuts me down. She'll tell me that no one, especially me, should criticize him because he is the hardest-working man on the planet. Mother is a terrible listener, and, like Dad, she can be very critical, to the point of reducing me and others to tears. She's constantly giving me advice I don't need, and she is easily offended when I don't agree with her." Sighing heavily, she said, "I dread being around either of them for any extended period of time. They are so overwhelming!"

Shannon explained that her bitter feelings toward her parents had been rising for the past several years because of the ways she felt manipulated each time they visited her home. "They want to be known as super grandparents," she explained, "but I cannot tolerate the way they treat my kids. They have very different values from my husband and me, and they routinely tell me that they disapprove of my standards. As a simple example, I have a set bedtime for the kids, and we try to keep a fairly predictable routine during the school year so they can get proper rest and stay on top of their assignments. I honestly don't think I'm rigid; I just feel that some measure of organization is good for the family. My mother sometimes pops in fairly late on school evenings and wants to take one of the kids shopping. She might buy my twelve-year-old daughter outrageous outfits that are about one step above the standards of a streetwalker. I'll tell Mom that I don't want her to go out shopping on a school night, and furthermore, I'd like to have input on the clothes she buys, because I don't trust what she'll bring home. In front of my kids, she'll accuse me of living in the Dark Ages, and she'll scold me for being too conservative. She's constantly undercutting my values, and nothing I say gets her to stop. Once she has a point to make she'll rattle on and on."

Shannon told me about many memories of being shamed by both of her parents. She explained how weary she was of their tendency to interrupt her when she had something to say, and she was tired of the many ways they intruded on her life, with little regard for the day's schedule. "My parents seem to live in their own bubble," she said, "where nothing matters beyond their own whims and demands. I don't know anyone else who is so oblivious to another person's needs."

In one of our discussions, I mentioned to Shannon that she had made the mistake of continuing to respond to her parents by complaining and arguing, much as she had done as a teenager. She was getting the same poor results as she did in those earlier years. Their volatile relationship was typified by ugly accusations and debates that went nowhere. It was time to do things differently.

Over the course of several weeks, in our sessions Shannon and I focused on rooting out her anger that had been mismanaged for so many years. We discussed the concept of choices (as outlined in

Chapter Six), and we talked extensively about how she no longer had to be intimidated by their overwhelming ways, nor did she have to win any debate. She could stop suppressing her anger and explain clearly how she intended to manage her household. When her parents proved to be too intrusive, she could invite them to leave. She was under no obligation to dance with them in this unhealthy relationship.

In time, Shannon felt increasingly emboldened to confront her parents about their narcissistic behaviors, and for the first time in their relationship, she stopped playing the role of argumentative girl and became a full-fledged adult. Her parents predictably did not like her new resolve, but she determined that she did not have to maintain their approval. Rather, she needed to be true to herself, even if it meant being misinterpreted by her parents.

Narcissists have a way of wearing out those closest to them. The constant battle to calculate responses to narcissistic demands, and the probability that the wrong behavior will be met with derision, scorn, or correction is corrosive. If you feel that you have to deliberate carefully about how to speak or act to avoid making a fatal mistake that will trigger the narcissist's absurd reactions, it's natural that you would come to feel deeply resentful. As weeks turn into months and years, this weariness can eventually become fuel for simmering bitterness that will not die easily—and that damages you without changing the narcissist at all.

Many of us who have regular contact with narcissists do not have the luxury of simply walking away, choosing never to see them again. Often the narcissist is a spouse, a close family member, someone in the same social circle, or a business associate whom you will encounter fairly regularly. As desirable as it may seem to retreat permanently from such a person, it might not be logistically possible. Given the fact that a narcissist will make little real change, it's necessary to find a way out of bitterness and anger and into a more balanced and life-sustaining response. The key to that way is, in my view, forgiveness.

## Another Way: Forgiveness

It might seem to you that forgiveness is an impossible feat for those who are in protracted relationships with narcissists. Many people struggle to forgive narcissists because they have such a deep history of feeling mistreated, and there is a strong likelihood that the mistreatment will recur in the future. "If I forgive," they may reason, "it would feel like I am conceding victory to the person who has done wrong." Forgiveness can seem too good for a narcissist, given the lack of remorse or the extensiveness of the damage that person created. But the reality is that even when you learn the ways of managing narcissists that we have discussed in this book—managing your anger, removing fear from the interactions, practicing humility, and fostering your own inner security—you might still feel bitter and resentful that the narcissist cannot and will not change. Forgiveness is the only thing that will truly bring balance to your spirit as you continue to relate with these deeply troubled and troubling people.

Even though Shannon, through our counseling sessions, learned to stop her enabling behaviors and became more assertive and independent, she was still not sure what to do with the bitterness and resentment that had built up over the years. "Mother and Dad are still selfish people," she told me, "but at least I am not being a pushover like I was in the past, and I've been much more consistent in communicating that they cannot take over my parenting role when they show up at my house." She sighed deeply as she added, "I still need to figure out what to do with the feelings of resentment that have built up over the years. It doesn't take much to remind me of how badly I hurt due to their many exploits." We had discussed forgiveness as a way of balancing and managing her negative feelings, but she was now realizing that forgiveness would not be easy or natural.

I mentioned to Shannon that as she determined to forgive, it would be necessary to understand what forgiveness is and what it is not. We discussed several thoughts along those lines. Contrary to popular belief, forgiveness does not comprise any of the following:

- Denying the legitimate pain you have experienced
- Agreeing to act like best friends with the person who has done you wrong
- Not feeling legitimate anger
- Allowing others to continue to disrespect your needs and boundaries
- Condoning behavior that is clearly inappropriate
- Telling the wrongdoer that the past is irrelevant and that it is okay to pretend as if nothing ever happened
- Ignoring the ill effects of past wrongs that continue to influence current events

When you forgive, it does not mean that you stop being assertive; nor does it imply that you have "gone soft" about the problems that have left deep wounds. Forgiveness *does* mean that you are willing to let go of harmful or ineffective forms of anger and are choosing to turn over the ultimate resolution of wrongdoings to God.

Shannon and I discussed the positive aspects of forgiveness:

- It frees you to focus on the priorities that are more important than anger.
- It prompts you to let go of obsessions about the one who has wronged you.
- It compels you to stop making insulting and derogatory remarks about the one who has done wrong.
- It causes you to be forward looking about your life's course.
- It causes you to put acceptance and tolerance first.
- It reminds you that you cannot control another person's choices.

Shannon had legitimate reasons to harbor negative feelings toward both parents, if she were so inclined. They were quite shallow. They had a deep track record of ruining important dates like birthdays or holidays. They often talked about her behind her back. Any gestures of friendliness often foreshadowed their requests for favored treatment. They used money to manipulate her children. They often gave advice that she did not want or need, but rarely listened to her advice in return. When she became assertive, they routinely punished her with silence. They were often secretive. Knowing these things, I mentioned to her, "There is no doubt that you have been on the receiving end of a raw deal. Forgiveness can seem like you are letting them off the hook too easily, so we are going to need to decipher good reasons for doing so."

As we discussed forgiveness, I told Shannon, "We're trying to find a delicate balance in the ways to respond to your parents. Because they are not going to exit your life in the foreseeable future, they will be a fixture to deal with. Your assertiveness will certainly serve you well as you show them a new you. Unfortunately, that assertiveness won't erase all the feelings of aggravation that have been building for decades, and that is where forgiveness comes in." As Shannon found out and I have learned in working with narcissists, this kind of forgiveness has several components.

### Choose Forgiveness

As people such as Shannon turn toward forgiving the narcissists in their lives, they often make a major mistake in assuming that they are *supposed to* forgive. In the words of one man who spoke with me about forgiving a caustic ex-wife, "Forgiveness is too good for her because she is so haughty and unrepentant, but my faith instructs me to be a forgiving person, so I guess that's what I have to do." I immediately knew he was not ready to forgive. Any effort to force forgiveness would merely be window dressing.

No one has to forgive a narcissist. You can always choose hate, bitterness, and resentment. Most narcissists have done enough wrong that those they have affected can certainly justify not forgiving them. By making forgiveness a choice rather than an obligation, we can begin to determine why we would choose to let go of painful emotions in the first place.

Shannon echoed many others' frustrations when she told me, "As I look back on my history with my parents, I can recall so many times when they were so selfishly insensitive to my needs that it takes no time at all for my blood to boil. How can they justify being so obnoxious? What rationalization could possibly make them feel good about being so critical and intrusive?" Her voice rose and her face flushed as she spoke.

Shannon wanted to forgive her parents, but she compounded her struggle when she focused on their unworthiness. I wanted to challenge her to use a different line of thinking, so I said, "Let's reposition your thoughts about forgiveness. First, let's establish that when you cling to bitterness, it is analogous to a situation where you drink poison and hope it will kill the other person." Shannon sat up straight in her chair as she quickly replied, "That would be absurd!" Grinning slightly, she nodded and said, "You're trying to get me to see that forgiveness is not something anyone can earn; it is done for my sake, not theirs." I nodded as I let the thought soak in, then I added, "You are under no obligation to forgive your parents, not now and not ten years from now. Decades of exposure to their destructive ways have created lots of emotional strain within you, and frankly, I don't blame you for feeling greatly annoyed."

Shannon quickly interjected, "Yeah, they really have been difficult, but I'm tired of feeling so wrung out when I deal with them. It's time for a new path."

"I happen to believe that falling back into the same old rut of bitterness will only produce the same old lousy results," came my reply. "I think you will be a much less tense person if you choose to forgive, but remember, that's a choice no one can make for you, and frankly, you'll need to do it for no other reason than it makes sense."

By seeing forgiveness as an option, people such as Shannon can contemplate it more deeply than if she had done it as a matter of moral or religious obligation. The forgiving person has to own the process from the inside out, not as a teaching that has been begrudgingly received. While each of us is free not to forgive, the benefits of forgiveness are clearer.

### Release Yourself from the Bondage of Pain

As bitterness and resentment build, so does bondage to emotional pain. Keep in mind that a primary goal of narcissists is control. Nothing pleases them more than knowing that they can dominate another's life. As they sense that others are feeling frustrated, they interpret that as proof that others cannot live without their advice and input. Your bitter anger empowers them to continue being overbearing, which then keeps you in their control—and in your painful emotions. It is a vicious cycle that can only be broken first by assertiveness, then by forgiveness.

When I spoke with Shannon about her bondage to pain, her eyes lit up as she remarked, "That describes the way I've felt for years. It seems that I'm constantly wondering what my parents will think if I do something outside their box. I know I shouldn't worry so much about what they think, but I've been so programmed to react that it feels odd to take my own initiatives. It is as though they have control over my mind."

"They have control over you only as you allow it," I responded. "When you were a child, you were heavily dependent on their input as you tried to make sense of your life. You are no longer in that position, and it is time that you seized the opportunity to become your own person."

Shannon thought a moment, then remarked, "I've known for a long time that I needed to separate from them, but the repercussions would be so predictably uncomfortable that I've procrastinated." Then, shaking her head, she said, "And in the meantime, I've become an emotional wreck. I've got to get out of this mess."

When you choose to forgive an antagonist, you simultaneously determine to remove the emotional shackles that have inhibited you from being the effective person you might otherwise be. People stuck in bitterness have handed over the controls to the narcissist, in effect saying, "I can't move forward until you behave better." This, of course, is a formula for disaster, since narcissists do not take direction from others. In contrast, when you forgive, you embody your belief that you can be emotionally healthy even without that person's cooperation. You're free.

### Affirm Your Self-Worth

In their behavior toward others, narcissists are basically saying, "Your feelings and needs are of so little value that I'll give no consideration to them. You don't matter." Narcissists have very low regard for anyone who thinks differently from them, and they are not bashful about showing their displeasure when someone counters them in any way. Few people meet their standards for acceptance, so they are constantly judging others—usually negatively. Those they judge can reel in self-doubt and insecurity.

When you respond to their rejection with bitterness, you have indicated that you believe that you cannot move forward in peace until you receive the narcissist's blessing, which will never come. It is futile to ask, "What will it take to make this person see that I am a decent person? How can I prove that I really do matter?" You are making the grave mistake of allowing your worth to be determined by one who knows little about true encouragement.

When I spoke with Shannon about the insulting covert messages she had received from her narcissistic parents, she nodded knowingly. "Ever since I was a child," she explained, "I have had questions about my value to them. I remember wondering at an early age why they were so easily upset with me. Nothing I did pleased them, but that certainly didn't stop me from trying to gain their approval. It seems like much of my life has consisted of bending over backwards to do what has to be done to get on their good side, but it is a never-ending quest. To this day, I wonder if they will get mad at me if I do the wrong thing. I know I shouldn't worry about those sorts of things, but I do. It bothers me greatly when they find fault with me."

Shannon's recent efforts to become more assertive were indications of her increased commitment to affirming herself and her worth. I told her, "When you have gone as far as you can with your assertions, the next step in affirming yourself is to stop expecting or asking your parents to approve of you. By forgiving, you illustrate that you believe in your innate worth whether they concur or not. Your choice to forgive shows that you accept their limitations. Regrettably, they do not know how to love fully, and certainly they do not understand the concept of unconditional acceptance. No amount of pleading or wishful thinking will change this. Your choice to forgive is your way of shifting gears for the purpose of building your self-esteem on a firmer foundation."

Narcissists are generally unaware. They do not comprehend some of the most fundamental truths about life, including the basic tenet that each individual brings positive qualities to relationships. They do not understand that relationships can be most satisfying when the participants affirm one another. They fail to grasp the joy that results from tapping into another person's positive traits, celebrating the good that can be found in others. Locked in a mindset that cannot see beyond personal cravings, they sadly live without the satisfaction of knowing that genuine happiness is a by-product of giving, not receiving.

When you forgive a narcissist, you openly acknowledge that person's limitations even as you also remember that you can value and affirm yourself without their awareness. By forgiving, you declare that the narcissist is not the final arbitrator of truth.

## Level the Playing Field

Relating with a narcissist can be similar to riding a seesaw—an ongoing game of one-up, one-down exchanges. Think of a recent time when you have attempted to discuss your own ideas with a narcissist. Was there respectful communications of beliefs and feelings? Most likely not. Instead, it was probably typified by put-downs, invalidating comments, interruptions, and insults. To them, interactions are not about gaining insights and awareness, but gaining the upper hand. Narcissists honestly believe that their antagonists are inferior and in need of their enlightenment.

Emotionally healthy individuals do not condescend to other people. They recognize that while we all differ in skills, experiences, and ideas, no one can claim personal superiority over another, and we are all equal. Differences are not turned into a referendum about comparative worth; rather, they are seen for what they are, indications that not all individuals think alike—nothing more, nothing less.

When you hold on to bitterness, you are still on the relationship seesaw with the narcissist, frustrated that you have not figured out how to gain the upper hand. Your bitterness can serve as a reminder that it is futile to relate either from the upper or the lower position in the relationship. When you reach the decision to forgive the narcissist, it will be your way of indicating that you no longer think of the relationship in competitive terms. Even when the narcissist insists on putting you in the lower position, you can choose not to respond with the extremes of shame or spitefulness, because your priorities will direct you toward tolerance and acceptance.

As Shannon made strides in handling her parents' criticisms, she noticed that they nonetheless continued to think negatively about her. They still balked and criticized. While she was tempted to question them about their haughty attitudes, history reminded her that they did not listen to anything that ran counter to their presumed wisdom. They were who they were, and they weren't about to be persuaded to become anything different. "As I have considered the option of forgiving them," she told me, "it dawned on me that they would never admit that they have treated me as an inferior all my life. I've decided that I still need to determine how to be wisest in my reactions toward them, and if they never get it, that's not my problem to solve."

By combining assertiveness with forgiveness, Shannon determined that she merited equal status, whether or not her parents agreed. She understood that their inability to change did not have to dampen her resolve. She was not being disrespectful by concluding that they were wrong to treat her as a lowly person. She was simply allowing her mind to be guided by a new perspective that they could not grasp.

## Release the Illusions

With the realization that forgiveness is necessary comes the loss of a dream. By forgiving, you acknowledge that wholeness cannot be found or restored. The relationship has proven to be incomplete, and no effort you make will remove the pain. Choosing to forgive implies that you recognize that broken feelings cannot be mended through normal channels of communication. Loose ends will always be a part of that relationship, and the emotional debt that has accumulated will never be repaid.

Shannon confessed to me, "In the past I kept hoping that things would eventually turn around in my relationship with my parents. I'd tell myself that surely as I aged and matured they would shift gears and treat me more as an adult, but that has not happened, and now I'm accepting that it never will. I guess you could say that I'm having to give up the hope that I could have normal relations with them." It was painful to admit, but her parents were never going to treat her with the dignity that a forty-year-old woman deserved. Their self-absorbed thinking kept them stuck in a rut that compelled them to ignore her needs, worrying only about maintaining their own agendas.

Holding on to bitterness makes it hard to come to terms with reality. We do not want to concede that someone could be so crass that they would repeatedly mistreat us. Our ideals might be noble, but they are also misguided. In a sense we become victims of our own common sense.

By choosing to forgive, Shannon was conceding that her parents would never appreciate or understand her good ideals for healthy relationships between parents and adult children. She was free to make plans that incorporated the regrettable truth that she could not afford to be too closely tied to her parents and that she should seek her emotional support from other sources. She told me, "I'm realizing that as long as I hoped that Mom and Dad would be supportive and encouraging, I was setting myself up for pain and disappointment. If I forgive them, though, it is my way of telling myself that I can move on, even if it means accepting that I'll never have an intact extended family."

Not being able to let go of bitterness gets us stuck in a childish approach toward life; we demand that significant others treat us well before we can be healthy ourselves. Like young children, we wonder in bewilderment why the outer world can be so cruel and unloving. The accompanying anger represents our demand that those unloving people meet our standards before we can move forward with life. Accepting forgiveness as the better path demonstrates the realization that the outer world does not owe anyone good treatment. We might prefer goodness, but we can make plans to be emotionally stable even in the presence of undesirable circumstances.

### Recognize the Inevitability of Pain

Imagine life with no pain. While that might seem great at first blush, it's really not the case. Suppose, for instance, that you have taken a bad fall and have broken bones in your ankle. If you felt no pain, you would get up and try to walk, oblivious to the damage to your ankle and the further deterioration that would follow. Without pain we don't have the body's warning mechanism that directs us toward taking care of ourselves and promoting healing.

Emotional pain can be understood as your personality's way of signaling that you need to change something so better feelings can surface. Rather than fearing pain, you can learn to read its messages wisely so you can use those insights to improve your life.

When you try—and fail—to alleviate painful feelings in dealing with a narcissist, you can either collapse under the weight of your emotional hurt or you can ask what that hurt is communicating. Often the hurt is telling what most people conclude: that participating in relationships with a narcissist is so futile that you are better off looking for more productive ways to expend your emotional energies.

"All my life I have felt hurt because of my parents' mistreatment, and often that hurt has been very intense," Shannon explained. "Now I can see that as I wallowed in the shame and anger that were by-products of such a toxic relationship, I have been the one to suffer most. It has caused me to be much less effective in the other relationships that I prize. My hurt is becoming a motivation to look for better ways to position myself in relationships, not just with my parents, but with anyone."

Though strange to acknowledge, suffering through relationships with narcissists can equip us to approach other relationships with greater depth than if we had never had the pain. While I never respond with glee when I hear of individuals being exposed to foul treatment at the hand of narcissists, neither do I cringe with defeat. When managed maturely, pain can propel change and health. Those who have been manipulated can powerfully resolve to approach life with anything but a repetition of those manipulations.

Being a mother of three children under twelve, Shannon naturally reflected on ways to apply lessons learned from her history with her parents. "If nothing else," she said, "I know what not to do as I handle problems with my own children. I can still remember how awful I felt, for instance, when my mother would embarrass me by screaming at me in front of my friends. Nothing can erase the hurt I felt, and maybe now that's not such a bad thing because, I can assure you, I'll never do the same when the opportunity presents itself in my kids' lives." She also described how she and her husband resolved to talk openly and sanely with their children about conflicts

or failures. They also were committed to making positive memories
with their children by having enjoyable family times. Likewise, they
taught their children the wisdom of paying compliments as opposed
to becoming a chronic critic. Their resolve toward such positive
parenting was a direct by-product of the pain Shannon had grown
up with in her family.

As Shannon stayed with her decision to forgive her parents, she
did not minimize the validity of her hurt and anger. Forgiveness allowed her to stop obsessing about what went wrong and allowed her
to focus instead on how she would be a better person. She summarized the process well by saying, "As I let go of my resentment toward
my parents, I'm showing that I get it. Life is more about learning how to love, not how to hate. I refuse to let them leave me with
a legacy of a bitter spirit." Shannon's pain has not been wasted.

### Move Toward Closure

When it comes to control and dominance, narcissists simply do not
give up. They are so impressed with their ideas and priorities that
they cannot believe that others wouldn't want to think and act
as they do. Their refusal to acknowledge others' priorities can keep
conflicts alive for years and years. That's what makes healing and
closure so difficult. Not only do they not initiate closure, their constantly critical and judgmental attitudes do not allow them to feel
peaceful toward those who dare to diverge from their directives.
That being the case, if closure is to be found when differences still
exist, it will have to come from someone other than the narcissist.
And closure is only possible as a by-product of forgiveness.

Through the years, Shannon learned that there was nothing
she could do to get her parents to accept and respect her unique approach toward life. Her parenting style differed from theirs, as did
her spiritual practices, her social inclinations, and even such daily
matters as how she prepared meals and managed family schedules.
Clearly she had chosen to break away from the family patterns she
grew up with. Her parents argued powerfully about how things

ought to be, and Shannon had traditionally either argued with them or collapsed under the pressure she felt from them. In counseling, when Shannon recognized that she had contributed to her own emotional pain when she failed to be true to her convictions, she committed to making needed changes to act independently. She determined to let her behavior accurately reflect her thoughts. She would no longer capitulate to her parents' narcissistic whining and criticism.

Predictably, as Shannon displayed her newfound confidence by being more decisive and separate, her parents expressed disappointment and dismay. For instance, one Saturday her parents asked if Shannon and her kids would join them for lunch at a favorite hamburger joint. Shannon had no particular plans that day, but she told her mother, "We've had such a hectic week that I think we need a day just to stay home and take care of the small things that need to be done around the house." Instead of being understanding, her mother poured on the guilt. "Do you mean that you don't have just one hour to spare for your own mother and father? Are you so selfish that you cannot alter your plans just a little?"

In the past Shannon would have agonized about the controversy she had created, but now she was in a different frame of mind. She calmly explained, "I certainly don't mean to give the impression that we don't care about you. We've simply been through a particularly tough week, and we need a break. I hope you'll be able to understand." Nothing more was said, although Shannon knew that her mother thought the explanation was insufficient.

Later Shannon explained to me, "I've come to the realization that Mom can't or won't help herself when she acts that way. I've spent too much of my life being angry with her, and I need to move away from chronic frustration. I am learning to accept her for what she is, and when she tries to manipulate me with false guilt, I forgive her. She's a troubled person who does not need my condemnation." Though her decision did nothing to change her mother's actions or attitudes, it represented a major breakthrough for Shannon. She was determined that she would not wallow in the emotional stench that so commonly accompanies such a relationship.

People who choose to forgive the narcissists demonstrate an inner strength that is anchored in a desire to give higher priority to peace and goodness. They show that they see themselves as entirely separate from the ones who would like nothing more than to own their thoughts. Forgiveness, then, cannot only be understood as a determination to move away from toxic-relating patterns; it is also an affirmation in your own belief that you deserve a way of life that is anchored in dignity.

## Two Mistakes to Avoid

When you indicate to a narcissist that you are not willing to be manipulated, that is likely to upset the narcissist because he or she knows no other way to relate. As the narcissist senses that you have excused yourself from exchanges with them, be prepared for a less than enthusiastic response. Often narcissists will use your resolve as an opportunity to further impugn your character. When this happens, there are two mistakes to avoid.

### 1. Refrain from Being Drawn into Rage

Shannon told me, "Ever since I was a little girl in Sunday School, I knew that forgiveness was a right thing to do. Even my mother, as much as she holds grudges, would reinforce the teaching that I should be big enough to know when to forgive. Now that I am learning to detach from her manipulations by forgiving, she seems greatly insulted. I'm honestly understanding that I can be a more balanced person by forgiving her, but as she sees me charting a new course, she becomes angry, sometimes to the point of rage."

When you make healthy adjustments in your responses to narcissists, they are likely to interpret your actions as attempts to gain the upper hand. They see everything as a competition, and when you choose not to play the loser, they become angry and threatened.

Nothing pleases a narcissist more than to be given an opportunity to rationalize their anger, and if you respond to their anger with anger, you give them a golden excuse to justify their rage. If you seethe with anger, they will sidestep personal responsibilities as they make your agitation the central issue. They can then conclude, "This proves once again how I am the better of the two."

As Shannon progressed in her counseling, she began to have less anger than pity toward her parents. "In the past," she told me, "I could match my parents' anger with my own unruly outbursts, and I'm sure that helped them feel justified for holding a low opinion of me. Now that I'm seeing the true virtues of forgiveness, I also see that they don't know what to do with me. They're angry that I won't respond like the rebellious kid anymore."

Narcissists will not be impressed by the contentment that accompanies your forgiving spirit, but you are not trying to impress them anyway. Let them stay angry. As you witness the inevitable misery that accompanies their choices, be glad that you are not stuck there with them.

## 2. Do Not Rescind Your Appropriate Assertions

While the goal of a forgiving person is inner peace, the goal of the narcissist is domination. As you consistently indicate that you are not going along with the narcissist, it is very likely that he or she will continue to give you reasons to show your resolve. Narcissists hope to generate enough fear in you so that doubt and uncertainty will prompt you to let them take control. They may repeatedly interrupt you or bully you or withdraw. They eagerly await the moment when you will say, "I really didn't mean it when I said I would live outside your boundaries. I'll comply."

Your commitment to forgiveness does not mean that you no longer will use assertiveness, only that your assertiveness will not give way to aggressive forms of anger. You are under no obligation to buckle under the pressure to resume the role of secondary citizen.

As Shannon continued being firm in her responses to her parents' intrusions, she occasionally questioned the wisdom of her newfound approach. "It's so out of the norm for me to be as strong with my parents as I have been lately," she confessed, "that it feels odd to be so bold. Sometimes it would be easier to just say nothing and let them bully me." But as quickly as she heard those words come from her mouth, she grinned and added, "But I'm not about to go back to the old way of being a mouse. That way sure didn't work!"

Living with a narcissist surely generates many feelings of sadness and grief, particularly if you are one who values friendship and cooperation. Despite such sadness, though, you do not have to apologize for your determination to live with your own guidelines. While it is understandable to lament the absence of good will, you do yourself no favors if you don't stand up for what you know is right and good.

In Shannon's case, she did all that she could to show her parents that she was available to engage lovingly with them. She called them regularly to just chat, she invited them to family functions, and she remained loyal to their family ties even when it would have been easier to just quit. She gave up the hope that they would appreciate her way of life, and she recognized that the relationship would remain shallow at best; yet she was satisfied that she would love them even if they did not share the same understanding of the nature of love.

As you consider the many interactions you will have with the narcissists in your life, you, like Shannon, can remain committed to the possibility of rewarding exchanges. At the same time, you can resolve that this commitment will not come at the price of your own personal well-being. Being true to successful living can have higher priority than making the narcissist comprehend what he or she cannot comprehend.

# The Author

After twenty-five years at the Minirth Clinic, Dr. Les Carter now maintains a private practice of counseling at the Southlake Psychiatric and Counseling Center in Southlake, Texas. He is the author or coauthor of more than twenty books, including *The Anger Trap, Grace and Divorce*, and *The Anger Workbook*. He speaks at conferences across the United States and can be reached at www.drlescarter.com.

# The Anger Trap
## Free Yourself from the Frustrations That Sabotage Your Life

LES CARTER, PH.D.

Paper
ISBN: 0-7879-6880-3

"The Anger Trap *is a masterfully written book, offering penetrating insights into the factors that can imprison individuals in unwanted patterns of frustration. With his well-developed insights and using case examples, Les Carter carefully explains how you can change your thinking, your communication, and your behavior as you release yourself from the ravages of anger gone bad.*"

—from the Foreword by Frank Minirth, M.D.

"*Les Carter has assimilated his years of experience counseling people trapped by anger into a book that I believe will prove helpful to many readers. The Anger Trap* offers fresh information and *understanding that can lead to recovery and reconciliation.*"

—Zig Ziglar, author and motivational speaker

"*The best book on anger out there. Five stars!*"

—Dr. Tim Clinton, president, American Association of Christian Counselors

Dr. Les Carter—a nationally recognized expert on the topics of conflict resolution, emotions, and spirituality, and coauthor of the bestselling *The Anger Workbook*—has written this practical book that strips away common myths and misconceptions to show viable ways to overcome unhealthy anger and improve relationships. With gentle spiritual wisdom and solid psychological research, Dr. Carter guides you to creating a better, happier life for yourself, your family, and your coworkers.

Les Carter, Ph.D., maintains his practice at the Southlake Psychiatry and Counseling Clinic in Southlake, Texas. Previously, Dr. Carter was with the Minirth Clinic for twenty-five years. He is a nationally recognized expert on topics including conflict resolution, emotions and spirituality, and marriage and family relationships. He is the author or coauthor of twenty books including the bestselling *The Anger Workbook, The Anger Trap, The Anger Workbook for Christian Parents*, and *The Freedom From Depression Workbook*. Dr. Carter can be reached at www.drlescarter.com.

Dr. Les Carter

*Grace and Divorce*

God's Healing Gift
to Those Whose Marriages
Fall Short

# Grace and Divorce

## God's Healing Gift to Those Whose Marriages Fall Short

LES CARTER, PH.D.

Hardcover
ISBN: 0–7879–7581–8

*"At last!* Grace and Divorce *achieves harmonious balance of biblical doctrine and biblical grace toward divorce. This is a very practical, user-friendly book that pastors, counselors, and church leaders will turn to again and again as they minister to hurting people."*

—Steve Grissom, founder, DivorceCare

*" . . . This book is long overdue. It will be an invaluable purchase, and a gift of grace, for those experiencing both the pain of divorce and the disapproval of fellow believers."*

—Freda V. Crews, D.Min., Ph.D., host of the internationally
syndicated television program *Time for Hope*

Divorce rates for evangelical Christians are just as high as for any other segment of American society, but the experience is made even more painful by the judgmental attitudes divorcees encounter in their churches and from their clergy. By offering a deeper and more nuanced scriptural explanation of the role of grace (and humanity's need for it) in our understanding of divorce, *Grace and Divorce* seeks to uphold the ideals of marriage while emphasizing how love and acceptance can still be given to those whose marriages have not attained the ideal.

Les Carter, Ph.D., maintains his practice at the Southlake Psychiatry and Counseling Clinic in Southlake, Texas. Previously, Dr. Carter was with the Minirth Clinic for twenty-five years. He is a nationally recognized expert on topics including conflict resolution, emotions and spirituality, and marriage and family relationships. He is the author or coauthor of twenty books including the bestselling *The Anger Workbook, The Anger Trap, The Anger Workbook for Christian Parents,* and *The Freedom From Depression Workbook.* Dr. Carter can be reached at www.drlescarter.com.